R. Gupta's®

Uttarakhand
GENERAL KNOWLEDGE

A Concise Description of History, Geography,
Economy, Polity, Flora & Fauna, Culture & more...

Compiled & Edited by
RPH EDITORIAL BOARD

2020
EDITION

Ramesh Publishing House, NEW DELHI

Published by:
O.P. Gupta *for* Ramesh Publishing House

Admin. Office:
12-H, New Daryaganj Road, Opp. Officers' Mess,
New Delhi-110002 ✆ 23261567, 23275224, 23275124

E-mail: info@rameshpublishinghouse.com
Website: www.rameshpublishinghouse.com

Showroom:
● Balaji Market, Nai Sarak, Delhi-6 ✆ 23253720, 23282525
● 4457, Nai Sarak, Delhi-6, ✆ 23918938

Book Code: R-469

ISBN: 978-93-86298-58-4

HSN Code: 49011010

CONTENTS

1. Uttarakhand : A Brief Introduction -------- 1
New Important Facts; A Special Category State.

2. History -------- 8
Chronology of events from Struggle to Formation; The Martyrs of Uttaranchal Struggle Movements.

3. Physical Features, Climate and Soil ------- 13
Physical features; Glaciers; Famous Vales; Climate; Soils.

4. Government ------- 18
Executive; Legislature; Constituencies at a Glance; Judiciary; Other Units of Administration; Districts, Tehsils and Blocks.

5. Economy ------- 26
Growing Economy, Resources of Uttarakhand; Inequalities in the Uttarakhand Economy.

6. State Finances ------- 31
Municipal Finances

7. Industries ------- 36
Industrial Policy, Types of Industries, Agro and Food Processing Industries; Biotechnology, Information and Communication Technology; Forest Products—Herbs and Spices; Tourism, Handicrafts, Handlooms, Industrial Areas/Estates/Parks.

8. Mineral Resources ------ 43
Brief Description of Minerals.

9. Agriculture, Horticulture & Fishing ------ 47
Land Distribution; Live Stock; Horticulture; Fishing.

10. Energy ------ 53
Start of Hydroelectric Projects; Commissioned Projects; Projects under Construction; Projects under Construction but Heldup; Chibro Power Plant (4 × 60MW).

(iv)

11.	**Irrigation**	56
12.	**Migration**	58
13.	**Growth in Uttarakhand : The Past and the Future**	60
14.	**Tourism** *Ministry of Tourism; Major Tourist Attractions; Nature Tourism; Pilgrimage Tourism; Adventure Tourism*	62
15.	**Char Dham Yatra** *Lakhamandal; Suryakund; Jankichatti; Hanumanchatti; Sayanachatti; Chamba; Barkot; Narendra Nagar; Gangotri (The Eternal Gift of Bhagirathi Penance); Gangotri Temple; Submerged Shivling; Gaumukh; Dayara Bugyal; Nandanvan Tapovan; Kedartal; Har-ki-doon; Uttarkashi; Maneri; Harsil; Sattal; Gangnani; Lanka; Dodital; Nachiketa tal; Bhaironghati; Kedarnath (The Celestial Jyotirlingam); Kedarnath Temple; Shankaracharya Samadhi; Gandhi Sarovar-chorebari Lake; Vasukital; Gaurikund; Sonprayag; Guptkashi; Agastmuni; Ukhimath; Kalimath; Chopta; Triyuginarayan; Panch Kedar (The other four Kedars); Badrinath; Narad Kund; Tapt Kund; Shesnetre; Neelkanth Peak; Brahma Kapal; Chandrapaduka; Panch Dharas and Panch Shilas; Urvashi Temple; Mata Murti Temple; Mana Village; Saraswati; Alka Puri; Satopath Lake; Bhimpul-Bhim's Bridge; Vasundhara Falls; Govind Ghat; Swargarohan Mountain; Joshimath; Panch Badris (the other four Badris); Panchprayag.*	68
16.	**Famous Temples** *Haridwar; Rishikesh; Almora; Ranikhet; Dehradun; Badrinath; Kedarnath; Chamoli; Uttarkashi.*	102
17.	**Famous Religious, Historical and Tourist Spots** *Haridwar; Kalsi; Badrinath; Kedarnath; Gangotri; Yamunotri; Nainital; Almora; Ranikhet; Kausani; Mussourie; Dehradun; Rishikesh; Lansdowne; Pindari Glacier; Religious and Tourist Spots of Uttarakhand: At a Glance; Cities of Uttarakhand..*	106
18.	**Famous Fairs and Festivals** *Famous Fairs of Uttarakhand; Festivals; Other Festivals; Fairs and Festivals : At a Glance.*	120

(v)

19. Forests, Animals and Birds ------- 124
Forests; Animals & Birds; Other Animals & Birds.

20. Rivers and Lakes ------- 130
Famous Rivers; Famous Cities of State Situated on the Banks of Rivers; Lakes; Chief Canals of the State; Chief Dams of Uttarakhand; Five Prayags; Mountain Ranges of Uttarakhand.

21. National Parks and Sanctuaries ------- 135
National Parks of Uttarakhand-At a Glance; WildLife Sanctuaries of Uttarakhand : At a Glance.

22. Scheduled Castes and Tribes ------- 137
Scheduled Castes of the State; Scheduled Tribes of the State.

23. Education System ------- 141
Universities; Research Organisations and Institutes; Famous Schools of Uttarakhand; Government Polytechnics; Literacy; Literacy Rate of Uttarakhand from 1951-2011; Districtwise Population of Male & Female; Literates and Literacy Rate.

24. Population and Area ------- 145

25. Art and Culture ------- 150
Folk Music; Folk Dance; Important Dialects of Uttarakhand; Painting.

26. Transportation ------- 152
Means of Transportation; Road Transport; Rail Transport; Air Transport; Water Transport.

27. First in the State ------- 155

28. Miscellaneous ------- 156
Uttarakhand State Public Service Commission; Law and Order in Uttarakhand; Uttarakhand Planning Commission; Abolition of Child Labour; Uttarakhand : Sports; Society, Women Welfare and Child Development; Names of Residential Units.

29. Personalities ------- 160
Great Personalities of the Past; Other Great Personalities.

Multiple Choice-Questions ------- 164

❑❑❑

STATE GOVERNMENT

**Trivendra Singh
Rawat**

Governor : Baby Rani Maurya   **Speaker :** Premchand Aggarwal

CHIEF MINISTER

✦ **Trivendra Singh : ** Home, Confidential, Personel, Vigilance, Law & Justice,
Rawat Secretariat Administration, General Administration, Suraaj,
Corruption Eradication & Public Service, Public Grievance,
State Property, Public Works, Rural Development,
Information, Rural Works, Rural Roads & Drainage, Civil
Aviation, Energy, Alternative Energy, Medical Services,
Medical Education, Family Welfare, Finance, Commercial
Tax, Revenue & Land Management and all other
Departments that are not allocated to other Ministers.

CABINET MINISTERS

✦ **Satpal Maharaj :** Irrigation, Flood Control, Minor Irrigation, Rain Water
Harvesting, Water Management, Indo-Nepal-Uttarakhand
River Projects, Tourism, Pilgrimage and Religious Fairs, Culture.

✦ **Harak Singh** : Forests and Wildlife, Environmental and Solid Waste
Rawat Disposal, Labour, Employment, Industrial Training, Ayush,
Ayush Education.

✦ **Madan Kaushik :** Urban Development, Housing, Rajiv Gandhi Urban Housing
Development, Census, Reorganisation, Elections.

✦ **Yashpal Arya** : Transportation, Social Welfare, Minority Welfare, Students
Welfare, Rural Ponds Development, Remote Areas
Development, Sub-Divisional Development and
Management, Backward Areas Development.

✦ **Arvind Pandey** : School Education, Adult Education, Sanskrit Education, Sports,
Youth Welfare, Panchayati Raj.

✦ **Subodh Uniyal** : Agriculture, Agricultural Marketing, Agricultural Processing,
Agricultural Education, Plantation and Horticulture, Silk
Development.

MINISTERS OF STATE (Independent Charge)

✦ **Rekha Arya** : Womens Welfare and Child Development, Animal
Husbandry, Sheep and Goat Husbandry, Fodder and
Meadows Development, Fisheries.

✦ **Dhan Singh** : Co-operatives, Higher Education, Dairy Development,
Rawat Protocol.

(vi)

MEMBERS OF LEGISLATIVE ASSEMBLY (Election-2017)

Constituency	Name (Party)	Constituency	Name (Party)
1. Purola (SC)	Rajkumar (INC)	37. Pauri (SC)	Mukesh Singh Koli (BJP)
2. Yamunotri	Kedar Singh Rawat (BJP)	38. Srinagar	Dr. Dhan Singh Rawat (BJP)
3. Gangotri	Gopal Singh Rawat (BJP)	39. Chaubattakhal	Satpal Maharaj (BJP)
4. Badrinath	Mahendra Bhatt (BJP)	40. Lansdowne	Dilip Singh Rawat (BJP)
5. Tharali (SC)	Munni Devi (BJP)	41. Kotdwar	Dr. Harak Singh Rawat (BJP)
6. Karnprayag	Surendra Singh Negi (BJP)	42. Dharchula	Harish Singh Dhami (INC)
7. Kedarnath	Manoj Rawat (INC)	43. Didihat	Bishan Singh Chauphal (BJP)
8. Rudraprayag	Bharat Singh (BJP)	44. Pithoragarh	—
9. Ghansali (SC)	Shakti Lal Shah (BJP)	45. Gangolihat (SC)	Mina Gangola (BJP)
10. Devprayag	Vinod Kandari (BJP)	46. Kapkot	Balwant Singh Bhauryal (BJP)
11. Narendranagar	Subodh Uniyal (BJP)	47. Bageshwar (SC)	Chandan Ram Dass (BJP)
12. Pratapnagar	Vijay Singh Panwar (BJP)	48. Dwarahat	Mahesh Singh Negi (BJP)
13. Tehri	Dhan Singh Negi (BJP)	49. Salt	Surendra Singh Jeena (BJP)
14. Dhanaulti	Pritam Singh Panwar (Independent)	50. Ranikhet	Karan Singh Mahara (INC)
15. Chakrata (SC)	Pritam Singh (INC)	51. Someshwar (SC)	Rekha Arya (BJP)
16. Vikasnagar	Munna Singh Chauhan (BJP)	52. Almora	Raghunath Singh Chauhan (BJP)
17. Sahaspur	Sahdev Singh Pundir (BJP)	53. Jageshwar	Govind Singh Kunjwal (INC)
18. Dharampur	Vinod Chamoli (BJP)	54. Lohaghat	Puran Singh Phartyal (BJP)
19. Raipur	Umesh Sharma Kau (BJP)	55. Champawat	Kailash Chandra Gahtori (BJP)
20. Rajpur Road (SC)	Khajan Dass (BJP)	56. Lalkuan	Naveen Chandra Dumka (BJP)
21. Dehradun Cantt.	Harbans Kapoor (BJP)	57. Bhimtal	Ram Singh Kaira (Independent)
22. Mussoorie	Ganesh Joshi (BJP)	58. Nainital (SC)	Sanjiv Arya (BJP)
23. Doiwala	Trivendra Singh Rawat (BJP)	59. Haldwani	Dr. Indira Hridayesh (INC)
24. Rishikesh	Premchand Aggarwal (BJP)	60. Kaladhungi	Bansidhar Bhagat (BJP)
25. Haridwar	Madan Kaushik (BJP)	61. Ramnagar	Diwan Singh Bisht (BJP)
26. BHEL Ranipur	Adesh Chauhan (BJP)	62. Jaspur	Adesh Singh Chauhan (INC)
27. Jwalapur (SC)	Suresh Rathor (BJP)	63. Kashipur	Harbhajan Singh Cheema (BJP)
28. Bhagwanpur (SC)	Mamta Rakesh (INC)	64. Bajpur (SC)	Yashpal Arya (BJP)
29. Jhabrera (SC)	Desraj Karanwal (BJP)	65. Gadarpur	Arvind Pandey (BJP)
30. Piran Kaliyar	Furqan Ahmad (INC)	66. Rudrapur	Rajkumar Thukral (BJP)
31. Roorkee	Pradeep Batra (BJP)	67. Kichha	Rajesh Shukla (BJP)
32. Khanpur	Kunwar Parnav Singh 'Champion' (BJP)	68. Sitarganj	Saurabh Bahuguna (BJP)
33. Manglaur	Qazi Mohd. Nizamuddin (INC)	69. Nanakmatta (ST)	Dr. Prem Singh Rana (BJP)
34. Laksar	Sanjay Gupta (BJP)	70. Khatima	Pushkar Singh Dhami (BJP)
35. Haridwar Rural	Yatishwaranand (BJP)		
36. Yamkeshwar	Ritu Khanduri Bhushan (BJP)		

CURRENT AFFAIRS

BUDGET 2019-20

The Finanace Minister of Uttarakhand, Prakash Pant on February 18, 2019 presented budget for 2019-20 in State Assembly. He announced interest-free loans of up to ₹ 1 lakh to poor and small farmers in the ₹ 48,663-crore budget. Interest free loan up to ₹ 5 lakh to self-help groups engaged in agro-related activities was also announced in the budget which focuses on agriculture and allied sectors, and rural employment. Tabling the state's budget, Finance Minister said it was a balanced budget which took care of education, health, agriculture, employment generation in rural areas, infrastructure, housing and urban development. The total expenditure for the Financial Year 2019-20 is estimated to be ₹ 48,663.90 crore while total receipts for the period are pegged at ₹ 48,679.43 crore which means it is a surplus budget, he said. The budget size is around 7 per cent more than the one passed last year.

BUDGET HIGHLIGHTS

- Interest free loans upto ₹ 1 lakh for agro processing and agricultural works to the poor farmers.
- Interest free loans to self-help groups upto rupees five lakhs for agricultural activities for the promotion of agriculture.
- 104.12 crores allotted to double the income of farmers by 2022, under the traditional agricultural development scheme.
- ₹ 150 crore for Atal Ayushman Uttarakhand scheme.
- Provision of four crore rupees under special incentive scheme for women entrepreneurs.
- The establishment of Law University in the state is budgeted at rupees 50 crore.
- ₹ 15 crore for Girls, 75 crore to Nanda Gauri Yojana.
- ₹ 67 crore under the Kaushal Vikas Yojana, a provision of ₹ 3.86 crores for the skill development scheme of women and weaker sections.
- ₹ 15 crore under self-employment in tourism under Vir Chandra Singh Garhwali scheme.
- ₹ 900 crore under Prime Minister's Gram Sadak Yojna.
- Approval of Asian Development Bank-approved 1400 crore for improving power system in the state.
- ₹ 121 crore provision for the construction of canals in unirrigated areas.
- ₹ 7 crore for construction and upgradation of Chief Minister Anganwadi centres.

1 Uttarakhand : A Brief Introduction

❑ Formation Day	:	November 9, 2000 (with name Uttaranchal as the 27th state of the country)
❑ Name change from the Uttaranchal to Uttarakhand	:	January 1, 2007
❑ Capital	:	Dehradun (Temporary)
❑ High Court	:	Nainital (Temporary)

❏ Geographical Position	:	28° 43' North to 31° 27' and 77° 34' East longitude to 81° 02'
❏ Geographical Boundary	:	Nepal in the East, Haryana and Himachal Pradesh in the West, Himachal Pradesh and China in the North, UP in the South
❏ Area	:	53,483 sq. km
❏ Length	:	From east to west 358 km
❏ Width	:	From north to south 320 km
❏ Commissionaries	:	Kumaon, Garhwal
❏ Number of Districts	:	13 (Nainital, Almora, Pithoragarh, Pauri Garhwal, Tehri-Garhwal, Uttarkashi, Chamoli, Dehradun, Udham Singh Nagar, Bageshwar, Champawat, Rudraprayag and Haridwar
❏ No. of Villages (2011)	:	16,793
❏ Number of Cities	:	92
❏ Legislative Assembly	:	Unicameral (Vidhan Sabha)
❏ Number of seats in present Assembly	:	70 (1 M.L.A. From Anglo Indian Society nominated by Governor, Total 71 M.L.A.)
❏ Number of members for Lok Sabha	:	5 (Garhwal, Almora (Reserved), Tehri, Nainital and Haridwar)
❏ Number of members for Rajya Sabha	:	3
❏ Position in Country according to area	:	19th
❏ State Animal	:	Musk-deer
❏ State Bird	:	Monal
❏ State Tree	:	Buransh
❏ State Flower	:	Brahma Kamal
❏ State Sign	:	Three mountains series with the pillar of Emperor Ashoka at the head in a stamp of round size has been shown where as the waves of Ganga have shown underneath

❏ First Governor : Mr. Surjeet Singh Barnala

❏ First Chief Minister : Mr. Nityanand Swami

❏ First Speaker of Legislative Assembly : Mr. Prakash Pant

❏ First Chief Justice : Justice Ashok A. Desai

❏ First Chief Secretary : Mr. Ashok Kant Sharan

❏ First Director General of Police : Mr. Ajay Vikram Singh

❏ Account of Uttarakhand was opened : With Rs. 2,192.08 crore (on 9th Nov. 2000)

❏ Main Source of Income : Tourism, Forestry, Minerals, Gardening and Hydraulic Electric Projects

❏ Other Source of Income : Fruits, Flowers, Wool, Fodder, Fish and Mushroom, Silk and Musk

❏ Population (According to Year 2011 Census) : 1,00,86,292 Persons

❏ Male Population : 51,37,773

❏ Female Population : 49,48,519

❏ Sex Ratio : 963 (per one thousand males)

❏ Density of Population : 189 persons per square kilometre

❏ Position in the Country According to Population : 21st

❏ Population Growth Rate in a Decade (2001-2011) : 18.81%

❏ Total Literacy : 78.80%

❏ Male Literacy : 87.40%

❏ Female Literacy : 70.0%

❏ Number of Total Literate Persons : 6,880,953

❏ Number of Literate Males : 3,863,708

❏ Number of Literate Females : 3,017,245

❏ Highest Literate District of the State : Dehradun (Total literacy 84.20%)

❏ Lowest Literate District of the State : Udham Singh Nagar (Total literacy 73.10%)

❑ Position in the Country : 17th
   According to Literacy
❑ Income per Head (2016-17) : ₹ 1,61,102
❑ Biggest District in Area : Chamoli (8,030 sq. km)
❑ Smallest District in Area : Champawat (1,766 sq. km)
❑ Forest Area (2017) : 24,295 km^2
❑ Net Area Sown : 7,41,099 Hectare
❑ Irrigated Agricultural Lands : 337566 Hectare
❑ Main Tourist Spots : Nainital, Mussourie, Haridwar, Badrinath, Kedarnath, Gangotri, Yamunotri, Hemkund Saheb, Rishikesh, Ranikhet, Dehradun and Almora
❑ National Parks : 6 (Corbett, Nanda Devi, Phoolon Ki Ghati, Rajajee, Gangotri and Govind National Garden)
❑ Wildlife Sanctuaries : 7 (Kedarnath, Ascot, Sonanadi, Govind, Winsor, Mussourie and Nandhaur wildlife Sanctuaries)
❑ Total Metalled Road (2016-17) : 43,762
❑ Post Offices (2016-17) : 2,722
❑ Total Schools/Colleges (2015-16) : 23681
❑ State Universities (2015-16) : 11
❑ Private Universities (2015-16) : 11
❑ Deemed Universities (2015-16) : 3
❑ Main Folk Songs : Vadee-Vadin, Laag, Bhaila and Pandav
❑ Main Folk Dances : Jagar, Jhora, Chaufula, Tharaya, Jumailo and Bhotia-Raso
❑ Chief Industries : Furniture, Woollen Clothes, Paper Industries, Electronic Industries, Sticks of Word, Toys, Sports' Goods
❑ Districts having More than : Dehradun (Population-16,96,694)
   15 Lakh Population   Haridwar (Population-18,90,422)
                         Udham Singh Nagar (Population-16,48,902)

❑ Airports : Pantnagar (Udham Singh Nagar), Jolly Grant (Dehradun), Naini Saini (Pithoragarh), Gauchar (Chamoli) and Chinyalisaur (Uttarkashi)

❑ Radio Stations : Almora, Pauri-Garhwal

❑ State Road Transport Corporation Area : Dehradun, Kumaon (Nainital)

❑ Main Languages : Hindi, Garhwali, Kumaoni, English

❑ Main Religions : Hinduism, Islam, Christianity, Sikhism, Buddhism, Jainism

❑ Monsoon Season : July–September

❑ Snowfall Season : December–February

❑ Main Crops : Wheat, Rice, Gram, Barley, Maize, Bajra, Peas

❑ Cash Crops : Sugarcane, Tea, Cotton, Sesame, Mustard, Tobacco, Groundnuts

❑ Main Fruits : Mango, Guava, Malta, Lemon, Black-berry, Orange, Apple, Litchi, Yam

Points to Remember

- State has been given special category by the Government of India on the recommendation of Planning Commission on 1st April, 2001.

- The newly formed 27th State of the country is the 11th State to have special category.

- According to mythology, Daksh Prajapati, son of Brahma started human race at Kankhal near Haridwar in Uttarakhand.

- One member each of 23 martyrs' families of Uttarakhand Movement have been honoured with government services.

- Hilly districts are–Nainital, Almora, Chamoli, Uttarkashi, Pithoragarh, Tehri Garhwal and Pauri Garhwal.

- Nainital Lake is situated in Nainital district.

- The names of Nainital City and Nainital Lake are possibly given on the name of Naina Devi Temple situated here.

- Tea plantation is done in Kumaon and Garhwal subdivisions in the middle of Himalayas and Shivalik mountains.

- Nainital and Dehradun districts are the most thickly tribal populated districts.

- The highest population of tribal people is found in Nainital district.

- The highest mountain range is Nanda Devi (in Chamoli district).

> About 45.32 per cent part of the beautiful Uttarakhand state is covered with forests. Out of a total 56.72 lakh hectare, only 7.41 lakh hectare land is cultivable, which counts for 13.06 per cent of the total area. The state is blessed with beautiful vallies and snow-clad peaks. The main characteristic of the state is bio-diversity, besides soil and environmental diversity, of this region. This is the reason that almost all types of important crops are cultivated here. The main crops are wheat, paddy, maize, manduwa and sanwa in food grains, urd, gram, pea, masoor, razma and gahath in pulses and mustard, soyabean, groundnut in oil seeds.

- The main vales situated in the North-East region of Garhwal district are—Dharma, Kingri-Wingri, Shailshal and Neeti, *etc.*

- Badrinath (Chamoli) city is a place for the re-establishment of Hinduism by Shankaracharya.

- Kumbh Fair takes place in Haridwar.

- Asbestos is received from Garhwal and Almora districts.

- Gypsum producing districts are—Garhwal, Dehradun and Nainital.

- Silver is received from the Almora district.

- The deepest lake of Kumaon region is Naukachhia Tal Lake.

- Dehradun Museum, Dehradun was founded in year 1914.

- Gurukul Kangri Museum, Haridwar was founded in year 1907-08.

- Annual Festival 'Sharadotsava' which is organised in Mussourie, Almora, Ranikhet, Pithoragarh and Chamoli districts, is recreational for foreign tourists as well as convalescing.

NEW IMPORTANT FACTS

- Dixit Commission has been constituted for the selection of permanent capital.

- The headquarters of State Properties, Food, Weight-Measurement and Consumer Protection, Election Office, Police Vigilance, Irrigation, Water Corporation, Treasury, Medical, Printing, Urban and Village Directorate *etc.*, departments have been established at Dehradun.

- Pro-tempore speaker Kazi Mohiuddin created a record of 46 days as pro-tempore speaker of Uttarakhand Legislative Assembly. Dharma Singh continued for 29 days as pro-tempore speaker of UP Legislative Assembly before it. Mr. Prakash Pant has honour to be first speaker of Uttarakhand Legislative Assembly.

A SPECIAL CATEGORY STATE

On 2nd May, 2001 it was decided in cabinet meeting to give special category status to Uttarakhand. It is applicable from 1st April, 2001. In this way, this newly formed state has become 11th state to have special category of state. The special category of states are—Sikkim, Jammu & Kashmir, Himachal Pradesh and seven States of east-northern regions. These states have been given special category of States according to Gadgil formula.

Special category is given to those states where density of population is low and those States are not economically developed and sensitive in their defence. The Central Government can provide special category to those states which are economically not sound.

Special category States get grants from the Central Government on special concessional rates. Now, Uttarakhand will get grants from the Central Government as 90% in the form of grant and 10% as debt whereas other States get 70% as grant and 30% as debt.

2 | History

KNOWN as Uttarakhand in ancient times now Uttarakhand-the place finds mention in the Hindu scriptures, the Vedas & Skanda Purana. Aptly referred to as Devbhumi or the Land of Gods, untouched & unexplored, the fagged rock faces have offered ideal meditation spots for holy men in their quest for the Creator. The Himalaya, believed to be the dwelling place of Lord Shiva–the destroyer among the three principal Gods of Hindu trinity has drawn travellers and mystics alike since time immemorial. The names 'Manas', 'Kedarkhand' and 'Kurmachal' are assigned to this place in Puranas.

Uttarakhand finds mention in the ancient Hindu scriptures as Kedarkhand, Manaskhand and Himavant. The Kushanas, Kunindas, Kanishka, Samudra Gupta, the Pauravas, Katuris, Palas, the Chandras and Panwars and the British have ruled it in turns. It has various holy places and abundant shrines.

Located in the foothills of the Himalayas, the State has international boundaries with China (Tibet) in the north and Nepal in the east. On its north-west lies Himachal Pradesh while on the south is Uttar Pradesh.

Words fail to describe the awesome charm and striking beauty of this magical land. Pictures do never tell the whole story of course. The splendor and the beauty of the land is to be seen and felt. Blessed with magnificent glaciers, sparkling and joyful milky rivers, gigantic and ecstatic Himalayan peaks, natural biospheres, valleys full of flowers, skiing slopes and dense forests, this abode of Gods includes many shrines and places of pilgrimage. This is the land where *Vedas* and *Shastras* were composed and where the great Indian epic Mahabharatha was written. The land has always been the source of inspiration for nature lovers and seekers of *peace* and *spirituality*.

Uttarakhand is a newly formed state in the north western part of India. The state was formed in 2000 and initially got the name Uttaranchal. In January 2007, the name of the state was officially changed from Uttaranchal to Uttarakhand, according to the wishes of a large section of its people.

Uttarakhand is both the new and traditional name of the state that was formed from the hill districts of Uttar Pradesh, India. Uttarakhand is also the ancient Puranic term for the central stretch of the Indian Himalayan containing some of Hinduism's most sacred pilgrimage spots. Literally *North Country* or *Section* in Sanskrit, its peaks and valleys were well known in ancient times as the abode of gods and source of Ganga (Ganges River).

The region was dominated by the Garhwal Kingdom in the west and the Kumaon kingdom in the east during the medieval period. In 1791, the expanding Gurkha Empire, current Nepal, overran Almora, the seat of the Kumaon kingdom. In 1803, the Garhwal kingdom also fell to the Gurkhas and became a part of Nepal. With the conclusion of the Anglo-Nepalese War in 1816, the Garhwal kingdom was reestablished from Tehri, and eastern *British* Garhwal and Kumaon ceded to the British as part of the Treaty of Sugauli.

In the post-independence period, the Tehri princely state was merged into Uttar Pradesh state, where Uttarakhand composed the Garhwal and Kumaon Divisions. Until 1998, Uttarakhand was the name most commonly used to refer to the region, as various political groups including most significantly the Uttarakhand Kranti Dal (Uttarakhand Revolutionary Party est. 1979), began agitating for separate statehood under its banner. Although the erstwhile hill kingdoms of Garhwal and Kumaon were traditional rivals with diverse lingual and cultural influences due to the proximity of different neighbouring ethnic groups, the inseparable and complementary nature of their geography, economy, culture, language and traditions created strong bonds between the two regions. These bonds formed the basis of the new political identity of Uttarakhand, which gained significant momentum in 1994, when demand for separate statehood (within the Union of India) achieved almost unanimous acceptance among the local populace as well as political parties at the national level.

However, the term *Uttaranchal* came into use when the BJP-led central government initiated a new round of state reorganization in 2000 and introduced its preferred name. Chosen for its allegedly less separatist connotations, the name change generated enormous controversy among the rank and file of the separate state activists who saw it as a political act, however they were not quite as successful as Jharkhand state that successfully thwarted a similar move to impose the name *Vananchal.* Nevertheless, the name Uttarakhand remained popular in the region, even while Uttaranchal was promulgated through official usage.

In August 2006, India's Union Cabinet assented to the four-year-old demand of the Uttaranchal state assembly and leading members of the Uttarakhand movement to rename Uttaranchal state as Uttarakhand. Legislation to that effect was passed by the State Legislative Assembly in October 2006, and the Union Cabinet brought in the bill in the winter session of Parliament. The bill was passed by Parliament and signed into law by the President in December 2006. Since then, Uttarakhand denotes a state in the Union of India.

Brave People: The people of Uttarakhand took part significantly in freedom struggle. 2334 jawans became martyrs of UP in the struggles after independence in which half were from Uttarakhand. There are more than 3 lakh ex-soldiers in Uttarakhand. There are two regiments of Uttarakhand in Indian Army–Kumaon and Garhwal regiments.

CHRONOLOGY OF EVENTS FROM STRUGGLE TO FORMATION

Movements for the formation of a new state continued for a very long time. Such movements actually starting before the independence. The long struggle for a state of Uttarakhand may be summarised in the following chronological order:

- To discuss the local problems, Kumaon Council was constituted in 1916 AD. The main functionaries were–Govind Vallabh Pant, Taradatta Garola and Badridatta Pandey.

- Jawaharlal Nehru extensively supported the right of hilly people for the development of their culture and to take decision according to their circumstances at the Congress session organised at Shrinagar of Garhwal region in 1938.

- In 1938 AD Shridev Suman organised 'Garhdesh Sewa Sangh'in Delhi which was later named as 'Himalaya Sewa Sangh'.

- It was demanded by Badridatta Pandey to Special Category to hilly region and constitution of separate unit for Kumaon-Garhwal by Ansuya Prasad Bahuguna at Haldwani-Conference in 1946.

- In 1950, after independence 'Hilly People's Development Committee' was constituted for greater Himalayan State (including Himachal and Uttarakhand).

- In 1955, Fazal Ali Commission recommended for the formation of separate State of hilly region.

- In June 1967, 'Hilly State Council' was formed under chairmanship of Dayakrishna Pandey, Deputy Chairman as Govind Singh Mehra and General Secretary as Narayan Datta Sundriyal.

- In 1970, P.C. Joshi formed 'Kumaon Rashtriya Morcha'.

- In 1979, 'Uttarakhand Kranti Dal' was formed at Mussourie for the demand of separate hilly State.
- In June, 1987 at Karnprayag, declaration of struggle for the formation of separate Uttarakhand State in All Parties Conference was made.
- In the Chairmanship of Shobhan Singh Jeema of BJP, 'Uttaranchal Progress Council' was constituted in 1988.
- 'In February, 1989, many organisations unitedly constituted 'Uttarakhand United Struggle Committee' for running of united movement for a separate State.
- In 1991, a proposal was passed by BJP Government in U.P. Legislative Assembly for formation of Separate Uttaranchal state and the proposal was sent to Central Government for acceptance.
- 'Kausik Committee' was constituted for the formation of Uttarakhand by the then Chief Minister Mulayam Singh Yadav.
- The People's movements of 1994 proved a mile-stone for the formation of Uttaranchal state. The leaders of U.K.D. kept fasting, wheel-jammed in the whole province and sabotages took place. Many people died at Khateema by police firing on agitators. The police tortured the agitators at Muzaffarnagar when they were going to New Delhi by buses. Many agitators died in dharna and procession at many places in the whole State.
- On 15th August, 1996, the then Prime Minister H.D. Dev Gowda declared the formation of Uttarakhand State from the Red Fort and a Bill was sent for the acceptance of U.P. Legislative Assembly.
- 27th July, 2000–The Government of India presented in Parliament the 'Uttar Pradesh Reconstitution Bill–2000'.
- August 2000–the aforesaid Bill was passed by the Lok Sabha and Rajya Sabha, the Bill was assented by the President of India.
- 9th November, 2000–the newly formed State of Uttaranchal, 27th State of Country, came into existence.

THE MARTYRS OF UTTARAKHAND STRUGGLE MOVEMENTS

Many agitators died at different places during Uttarakhand Struggle Movements. The names and important places where agitators became martyrs, are given below:

- The names of people killed in Khateema firing on Ist Sep., 1994 are–Pratap Singh, Paramjeet Singh, Bhuvan Singh, Dharmanand Bhatt, Rampal, Bhagwan Singh Sirola and Gopichand.

- The people killed in Mussourie firing on 2nd September, 1994 are–Balbir Singh Negi, Umashankar Tripathi, Dhanpat Singh, Belmati Chauhan, Raisingh Bangari, Hansa Dhanai, Guddu and Madan Mohan Manmagai.

- Many people were killed in police firing at Muzaffarnagar in U.P. when they were going to take part in a rally at Delhi on 2nd October, 1994. The name of few people who were killed in the firing are–Girish Kumar Bhadri, Satendra Singh, Ravinda Rawat Chauhan, Ashok Kumar Keshiv, Rajesh Lakhera and Suryaprakash Thapliyal.

- On 3rd October, 1994–in the agitation for the separate state, Pratap Singh Bisht at Nainital, Prithvi Singh Bisht and Rakesh Devarani at Kotwar and Rajesh Rawat, Deepak Walia and Balwant Singh Jangwar at Dehradun were killed.

3 | Physical Features, Climate and Soil

UTTARAKHAND is one of the frontier States of the country. Most parts of this State is hilly. For centuries, saints & pilgrims, braving hazards of climate & terrain, have walked these mystical vales in their search for the divine and seek salvation. The snowclad peaks & icy glaciers, life sustaining rivers, lush green valleys and an aura of spiritual serenity attracts people from all over the world also in search of adventure & challenges unmatched elsewhere.

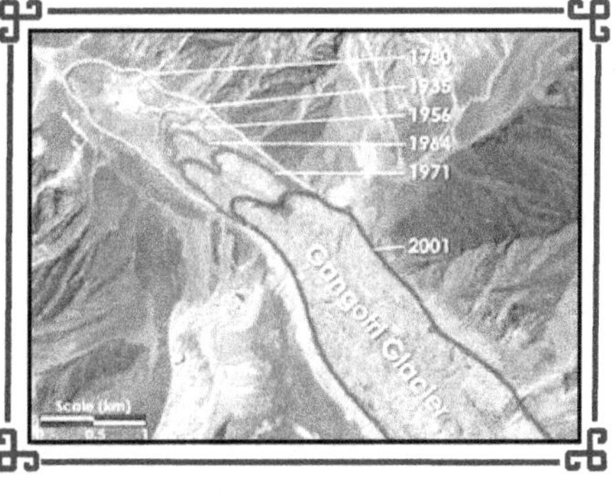

Uttarakhand is primarily a mountainous state with only about ten per cent of its total geographical area in the plains. Of the thirteen districts, Haridwar, Udham Singh Nagar and some parts of Dehradun and Nainital districts are in the plains, while the remaining areas of the state are hilly. Further, 90 per cent of its total population dependent on agriculture for the livelihood, the economy of Uttarakhand is predominantly dependent on mountain agriculture.

A special position is assigned to the state due to its earth structure, river-valleys, natural flora, diversity of surface divisions, beauty of mountain ranges, snow vales and glaciers. The state has traditionally been divided into two parts, the western half known as *Garhwal* and the eastern region as *Kumaon*. Uttarakhand derives from the Sanskrit for *North Country*. The State has been, divided geographically in three natural divisions:

1. Greater Himalayas
2. Middle Himalayas
3. Hills of Shivalik and Doon

1. Greater Himalayas : This natural sub-division is known as Himadri. This hilly part is extended 50 km in width whose most of the mountain ranges are 4,800 to 6,000 metre high. Many glaciers are found in this part. As a result, the sources of Bhagirathi, Alakhananda and Yamuna *etc.* are situated here. The soil of this part of Himalayas is made from the dregs of stones which is changed into valleys due to erosion.

The famous mountain ranges of this region are:

• NandaDevi	7,817 metres	• Trishul	7,120 metres
• Kamet	7,756 metres	• Doonagiri	7,066 metres
• Bander Punchh	6,315 metres	• Panchachuli	6,904 metres
• Mara	7,273 metres	• Nandakot	6,861 metres
• NandaDevi Eastern	7,434 metres	• Badrinath	7,138 metres
• Chaukhambha	7,138 metres		

Besides these, Kedarnath, Gangotri and Yamunotri *etc.* are glaciers whose heights are more than 6000 metres. This region is the coldest place because all the mountain ranges of this region are always covered with snow.

The area of Great Himalayas is hilly and uneven which is made of folded ranges in the shape of feathers. River Ganga drainage system, river Yamuna drainage system, Black river drainage system are present in this part. These river get water whole year from the glaciers present on the ranges of Greater Himalayas. River Ganga drainage System is present in almost all parts of this area except western

Greater Himalayas

part. The rainy season begins in this part mostly in the month of June and continues to the middle of September and its quantity is from 100 to 200 cm. It rains nominal in the winter season. A small quantity of rain falls in the form of snowfall. The rain which falls during summer is monsoonal type which does not go in the north because it can not cross the mountains.

Sub-tropical zonal evergreen florae are found in this part of Himalayas. The trees of Sar, Fir, Saal, Chir and Buihes and Grasses *etc.* are only found in more high areas. Florae are not found in the lower region of valleys of mountainous areas. The people of this area rear animals and agriculture is done only in the lower part of the valleys.

2. Middle Himalayas : This mountainous part of Himalayas is situated in the south of Greater Himalayas. The districts of Almora, Uttarkashi, Garhwal,

Tehri, Nainital *etc.* come in this area. The mountain ranges in this area are generally 3000 to 4000 metres high which are parallel to the chief ranges extended from east to west. In the middle of these-ranges, there are valleys at some places.

The middle Himalayas is very new part-according to its surface structure in which sedimental rocks are present. These sedimental rocks are seen in the form of plain fields in the areas which are nearabout 2000 metres high. There is intense cold in the middle Himalayan area in the winter. The temperature falls below the zero degree celsius. As a result, snow also falls whereas the weather in summer is pleasant. The average temperature of this season remains—between 18°C and 20°C. It rains heavily in the month of July due to summer monsoon. Its quantity raises upto 150 cm. Due to this, the water level of rivers rises in rainy season.

The coming and going of tourists continue in all parts of middle Himalayas in summer because the season of this part is colder than the other parts. Fifty per cent part of the middle Himalayas is covered with forests. The trees of Chir, Fir, Sal, Deodar *etc.* are mostly found in this area. These forests are very useful according to economical points of view because the woods of these forests are used for furniture making.

3. Hills of Shivalik and Doon : This part of Himalayas is also known as 'Foot of a mountain ranges' because these hills are situated in the south of Himalayas and comparatively of low height. The hills of Shivalik are very narrow from north-west to south-east and extended in the down side. Primarily these hills are extended parallel to the Himalayas. South Almora, middle of Nainital and Dehradun districts come under Shivalik area which are situated at the height of 750 m to 1500 m. These hills are quite different from Himalayas according to surface structure. There are less high hills in the south of Shivalik

---

THE HOLY HIMALAYAS

The Himalayas – the world's most majestic & loftiest mountain chain is the global heritage of all mankind. The sublime quality of this Abode of Snows' has, since time immemorial, inspired the sages & saints of India and has attracted tourists & pilgrims from world over to its awesome beauty & calm serenity. Uttaranchal abounds in places of sanctity where devotees converge every year to pay obeisance to their god's braving vagaries of weather and other human travails in Himalaya. Closest to the celestial beings, devotees from all corners of the country have flocked to these Himalayan shrines of Char Dham - Yamunotri, Gangotri, Kedarnath and Badrinath every year to seek salvation. The arduous trails remain in the ancient sanctuaries of faith for a fulfilling experience. The four dhams receive holy water in the form of four streams - Yamuna (Yamunotri), Bhagirathi (in Gangotri), Mandakini (in Kedarnath) and Alakhnanda (in Badrinath). Now the Himalayas are also a powerful magnet for those who come in ever increasing numbers from the world over in search of adventure and challenges unmatched elsewhere. Geologically speaking, the Himalaya is a young and still growing mountain range. 60 million years ago a plate of the earth's crust carrying the Indian land mass travelled 5,000 km from near the South Pole and collided with Laurasia, thus heaving up the Himalaya. The most substantial rise took place in the past 38 million years and the final thrust upward has occured in the past one million years. The tectonic forces that brought the Himalaya into being also created an extraordinary complex environment, exercising a very powerful influence upon the entire subcontinent. The mountain ranges are the major factor in determing the climate of India.

Hills of Shivalik and Doon

hills and many flat valleys are situated in the middle of small Himalayas. These valleys are called 'Doon'. This valley of Dehradun district is very important which is spread from 25 to 35 km in width and 350 to 750 metres in height. The valleys of Kota Doon, Patali Doon, Kothari Doon, Kiryana Doon *etc.* are situated near this valley.

The summer season in the regions of Shivalik hills and Doon hills is hotter than that of Himalayan–mountainous region. The temperature in this season remains from 28°C to 33°C, whereas the temperature in winter season remains from 4°C to 9°C. As a result, there is a snowfall in winter season in form of a little rain. It generally rains in rainy season and in summer season. The quantity of rain is from 150 cm to 220 cm. The weather is very pleasant in the areas of Mussourie, Ranikhet, Chakrata, Nainital *etc.* which are situated in Shivalik region. Therefore, people come to visit this terrain region. Natural florae are found in abundance in this region because trees of Sheesham, Amla, Saal, Chir, Deodar, Bamboo, Oak, Birch *etc.* are found in abundance which are very important for the economical point of view.

GLACIERS

S.No.	Glaciers	Districts
1.	Gangotri	Uttarkashi
2.	Milaan	Pithoragarh
3.	Poting	Pithoragarh
4.	Nabhik	Pithoragarh
5.	Pindari	Bageshwar
6.	Sundardhunga	Bageshwar
7.	Kafani	Bageshwar

FAMOUS VALES

S.No.	Vales	Connected areas
1.	Shringakantha	Uttarkashi-Himachal Pradesh
2.	Thaga-La	Uttarkashi-Tibet
3.	Muling-La (5669 m)	Uttarkashi-Tibet
4.	Bhara (Chirbatia or Dugari) La 5608 m)	Chamoli-Tibet
5.	Neeti (5044 m)	Chamoli-Tibet
6.	Barahoti	Chamoli-Pithoragarh
7.	Kungari-Wingari	Chamoli-Tibet
8.	Darma	Pithoragarh-Tibet
9.	Lipulekh	Pithoragarh-Tibet
10.	Trelpass	Bageshwar-Pithoragarh

CLIMATE

The climate of the state is generally temperate but varies greatly from tropical to severe cold, depending upon altitude. Different parts of the state experience temperature variations due to difference in elevation. Summers are pleasant in the hilly regions but in the Doon area, it can get very hot. It can get even hotter in the plains of the state. Temperature drops to below freezing point not only at high altitudes but also at places like Dehradun in the winters. Average rainfall experienced in the state is around 1079mm. Average temperature ranges between a minimum of 1.9°C and a maximum of 40.5°C.

SOILS

Five main types of soils are found in the state:

1. **Tertiary soil:** Found in Shivalik and Doon valley. This soil is suitable for production of tea.

2. **Cord soil:** The soil contains shell, cysts and quarts. This is light and unproductive soil found in Nainital district.

3. **Volcanic soil:** The soil is found in the mountain slopes of the state.

4. **Alluvial soil:** The soil is found in lower slopes of shivalik range and Dun Valley containing lime, iron and biological remains and is very suitable for agriculture.

5. **Grey Soil:** The major contents of this soil is lime but it is short of productive elements and it is found in Nainital, Mussorrie and Chakarata.

❖__❖__❖

4 | Government

ACCORDING to Indian Constitution, there is governorship and a unicameral Legislative Assembly in Uttarakhand. It is called a unicameral Legislative Assembly.

EXECUTIVE

The executive power of the state is kept in the hands of Governor which is used by him according to the Constitution of India or through his subordinate employees. The Governor is appointed by the President of India. He must be Indian citizen and must not be below 35 years in age. The Governor holds the office till the satisfaction of the President. The Governor is appointed for a fixed term of five years but may hold office until the next successor takes over.

The Governor is aided and assisted in the discharge of his functions by a Council of Ministers headed by a Chief Minister. The Governor is the chief executive Head of the State. The Council of Ministers is collectively responsible to the Legislative Assembly of the State. The Governor is a mere constitutional head of the State and the real and effective authority with respect to administration of the State is exercised by the Chief Minister and his Council of Ministers. Theoretically, the Governor is the executive head of the State and the Council of Ministers is an advisory committee.

The Governor of a state is responsible for the smooth functioning of the state administration. But, practically, he only supports the decisions of the ministers. He may influence the Council of Ministers according to his personality. The real executive powers are in the hands of the Council of Ministers and takes important decisions accordingly. Theoretically, the Governor is not bound to accept the advice of the Council of Ministers but he can not ignore the advice. The reason for it is that the Chief Minister is the leader of the major party in the Legislative Assembly and ignoring his advice may create Constitutional problems. Due to this reason, the Governor administers according to the Council of Ministers. The

Governor appoints the Council of Ministers. According to the Constitution, they hold office at the pleasure of the Governor. But it does not mean that the Governor can dismiss a minister. The Council of Ministers is responsible to the Legislative Assembly and so long as the Council of Ministers has vote of confidence in the Legislative Assembly till then the Governor dares not to dismiss any minister. But the Governor can help the Council of Ministers according to his experience and ability for the smooth functioning and upgrading the State administration. According to Article 167 of the Constitution, the Governor has full right to know about the administration of the State. It is the duty of the Chief Minister to acquaint the Governor from time to time about the State administration. The Governor may ask the Chief Minister to present the decision taken by a minister before the Council of Ministers. If the Constitutional machinery fails in the State, the President may declare emergency in the State. In Such circumstances, he works as the representative of the President and he works according to his own discretion when he recommends President rule in the state and does not take any advice from the Council of Ministers.

The work of Cabinet is to make coordination among the different departments, determination of State policies, Control over State executive. The Chairman of each department is either a minister or a State minister. He is collectively or personally responsible to the State Legislative Assembly. The Chief Minister distributes the portfolios of the Cabinet.

The hierarcy of departments is destined in the following way :

Head of Department —Minister or State minister (there may be deputy minister to assist the minister in the department).

- Secretary or Additional Secretary or Joint Secretary according to necessity.
- Deputy Secretary (Departmental)
- Additional Secretary (Sub-departmental)
- Section Officer (Section)
- Assistants
- Upper Division Clerks
- Lower Division Clerks

These officers are organised and related to one anothers according to 'Post Hierarchical Process'. Sometimes, the Directorate or the Board of any department is related to post hierarchical process. For example, there are Education Management Office and Uttaranchal Pre-Secondary Board in Education Ministry. The Police department is related to Home Ministry. There is a Inspector-General in each province. There are D.I.G., S.S.P., or S.P. (in district), D.S.P.O., Inspector,

Sub-Inspector and other policemen for his help. Their main duty is to maintain law and order.

Commissionaries: The State is divided in two commissionaries. The head of commissionary is called commissioner. The head of a district is called, the District Magistrate. There are many ADM and SDM for his assistance. The head of a Tehsil is called the Tehsildar. There are an assistant Tehsildar, Kanungo and Patwari *etc.* for the help of a Tehsildar. They are mainly related to revenue.

LEGISLATURE

Every State has a legislature consisting of one House or two Houses according to Article 168 of the Constitution. The State legislature consists of the Governor and one or two Houses. The Lower House is known as Legislative Assembly (Vidhan Sabha) and the Upper House is called Legislative Council (Vidhan Parishad). Uttarakhand State Legislature is unicameral that is Legislative Assembly (Vidhan Sabha) only.

State Legislative Assembly (Vidhan Sabha) : The only House of the State is called Vidhan Sabha. All the members of the State Legislative Assembly are directly elected by the people of the State on the basis of adult franchise except the nominated members of Anglo-Indian community. The State is divided in many election constituencies according to geographical basis that the population of 75 thousand may not have more than one representative. The Legislative Assembly of each State consists of not more than 500 and not less than 60 member. There is also an arrangement to make necessary changes after each census in election constituencies at the wish of parliament.

In each constituency, one representative is elected. According to Article 332 of the Constitution, there are reserved constituencies for Scheduled Castes and Scheduled Tribes.

There are 70 members in Uttarakhand Legislative Assembly. The life span of State Legislative Assembly is five years. The Legislative Assembly can be dissolved sooner than its life of five years by the Governor on the recommendation of the Chief Minister. If the Legislative Assembly is not dissolved before its life span it continues for five years from its first session and it dissolves itself after five years. The parliament has right to extend its tenure for one year in case of emergency. After the end of emergency, this time may not be more than six months in any condition.

The Legislative Assembly elects two members as Speaker and Deputy Speaker.

1.	Purola (SC)	36.	Yamkeshwar
2.	Yamunotri	37.	Pauri (SC)
3.	Gangotri	38.	Srinagar
4.	Badrinath	39.	Chaubattakhal
5.	Tharali (SC)	40.	Lansdowne
6.	Karanprayag	41.	Kotdwar
7.	Kedarnath	42.	Dharchula
8.	Rudraprayag	43.	Didihat
9.	Ghansali (SC)	44.	Pithoragarh
10.	Deoprayag	45.	Gangolihat (SC)
11.	Narendranagar	46.	Kapkote
12.	Pratap Nagar	47.	Bageshwar (SC)
13.	Tehri	48.	Dwarahat
14.	Dhanolti	49.	Salt
15.	Chakrata (ST)	50.	Ranikhet
16.	Vikasnagar	51.	Someshwar (SC)
17.	Sahaspur	52.	Almora
18.	Dharampur	53.	Jageshwar
19.	Raipur	54.	Lohaghat
20.	Rajpur Road (SC)	55.	Champawat
21.	Dehradun Cantt.	56.	LalKuwa
22.	Mussoorie	57.	Bhimtaal
23.	Doiwala	58.	Nainital (SC)
24.	Rishikesh	59.	Haldwani
25.	Haridwar	60.	Kalabhungi
26.	B.H.E.L Ranipur	61.	Ramnagar
27.	Jwalapur (SC)	62.	Jaspur
28.	Bhagwanpur (SC)	63.	Kashipur
29.	Jhabrera (SC)	64.	Bajpur (SC)
30.	Pirankaliyar	65.	Gadarpur
31.	Roorkee	66.	Rudrapur
32.	Khanpur	67.	Kichha
33.	Manglore	68.	Sitarganj
34.	Laksar	69.	Nanak Matta (ST)
35.	Haridwar Rural	70.	Khatima

JUDICIARY

There is a High Court in the State to settle the civil and criminal cases. The High Court of the State is situated at Nainital. There are District Courts and various subordinate courts under the Jurisdiction of High Court in the State. The State Judiciary is divided in two parts : First Uttarakhand Civil (Judicial) Service and second Uttarankhand Higher Judicial Service. In first come Munsif Magistrate, Assistant Judges and Civil Judge and in second come Civil and Session Judges (Now they called Additional District Session Judges). The State Judiciary is divided in districts which are under control of District Judges. In 1967, Judicial Judges (who were formerly under control of the government) came under the control of High Court. Consequently, the Judiciary was separated from the Executive except the revenue related matters.

The cases related to revenue are decided by the Collector or Additional or S.D.M. Their Jurisdictions are restricted. According to Indian Penal Code, the Nyay Panchayat has right to punish the offenders in petty criminal cases. The Nyay Panchayat can not send jail to the offenders.

Lok Adalats have also been constituted in Uttarakhand like other States of the country to provide free legal help. Uttarakhand Legal Help and Advisory Board has been constituted for its management and smooth functioning at State level. The units of the Board have been constituted in various districts which are called District Legal Help and Advisory Committees.

For the smooth functioning of the Lok Adalats, only those applicants can put their applications before the District Legal Help and Advisory Committee whose yearly income is less than poverty line. Although, there is no such restrictions on Scheduled Caste, Scheduled Tribe, women and soldiers. There are three bases of the functioning of these committees. Those are propaganda and expansion, to provide free legal aid and settle the dispute on the basis of compromise between the disputants to give them prompt justice and also give free legal consultations. Civil, criminal, consolidation, revenue, marriage and divorce, alimony and such other cases are settled in Lok-Adalats.

OTHER UNITS OF ADMINISTRATION

The State has been divided into two commissionaries for the convenience of administration, recovery of revenue and for the progress of development activities. The commissionaries have been divided into districts. There are 13 districts in

Uttarakhand at present. The districts have been divided into Tehsils and Blocks. The head of commissionaries and districts are called Commissioner and District Magistrate respectively.

District Councils have been constituted to manage the villages of Uttarakhand. The tenure of the Councils is for the five years. Only those persons can be the member of the District Councils who are eligible to vote for State Legislative Assembly and not less than 21 years of age. Such persons can not be elected for the District Council who are found guilty of sedition or any felony. There are a Chairman and a Deputy Chairman for the District Councils.

To maintain peace and harmony in the villages, Gram Panchayats are constituted by the elected panchas in the State. The heads of Gram Panchayats are called Sarpanch or Gram Pradhan. For their help, there are nearabout 5 panchas and nearabout 11 members. Just as the problems of villages are managed by the District Councils, in the same the civils amenities of cities are managed by the Municipalities. In big cities, these civil amenities are managed by the Municipal Corporations. The Municipalities are constituted in those cities whose populations are more than 20 thousand.

DISTRICTS, TEHSILS AND BLOCKS

Districts	Area (sq. km.)	Tehsils	Blocks
1	2	3	4
1. Almora **HQ:** Almora	3,144	1. Almora 2. Ranikhet 3. Bhikia Sain 4. Salt 5. Someshwar 6. Chakhutia 7. Dwarahat 8. Bhanouli 9. Janti 10. Syalde 11. Dhaul Dina	1. Dhauladevi, 2. Sult, 3. Syalde, 4. Bhikhiasain, 5.Tarikhet, 6. Dwarahat, 7. Chakhutia, 8. Lamgada, 9. Hawalbag, 10. Takula, 11. Bhansia Dina
2. Uttarkashi **HQ:** Uttarkashi	8,016	1. Dunda 2. Puraula 3. Bhatwari 4. Badkote 5. Chinyaliasaund 6. Mori	1. Bhatwari, 2. Dunda, 3. Chinyalisaund, 4. Naugaon, 5. Puraula, 6. Mori

Districts	Area (sq. km.)	Tehsils	Blocks
1	**2**	**3**	**4**
3. Udham Singh Nagar **HQ:** Udham Singh Ngr. (Rudrapur)	2,542	1. Kashipur 2. Kichchha 3. Khateema 4. Sitarganj 5. Jaspur 6. Bajpur 7. Gadarpur 8. Rudrapur	1. Kashipur, 2. Jaspur, 3. Bajpur, 4. Gadarpur, 5. Rudrapur, 6. Khateema 7. Sitarganj
4. Champawat **HQ:** Champawat	1,766	1. Champawat, 2. Pati 3. Purnagiri 4. Lohaghat 5. Poornagiri	1. Champawat, 2. Patee, 3. Lohaghat, 4. Barakot
5. Chamoli **HQ:** Gopeshwar	8,030	1. Chamoli 2. Joshimath 3. Karnaprayag 4. Tharali 5. Phokhari 6. Gairsann, 7. Ghat 8. Jilasu, 9. Adibadri	1. Joshimath, 2. Karnaprayag, 3. Narayan bagar, 4. Ghat, 5. Dasauli, 6. Tharali, 7. Deval, 8. Gairsann, 9. Pokhari
6. Tehri-Garhwal **HQ:** New Tehri	3,642	1. Tehri, 2. Pratapnagar 3. Devprayag 4. Narendranagar 5. Ghansali 6. Jakhnidhar 7. Dhanaulti, 8. Gaja 9. Kandisaund 10. Nainbag	1. Jaunpur, 2. Chamba, 3. Koldhar, 4. Tehri, 5. Pratapnagar, 6. Jakharidhar, 7. Ghansali, 8. Devprayag, 9. Kirtinagar, 10. Narendranagar
7. Dehradun **HQ:** Dehradun	3,088	1. Dehradun 2. Chakarata 3. Vikasnagar 4. Rishikesh, 5. Thyuni 6. Kalsi, 7. Doiwala	1. Doiwala, 2. Raipur, 3. Sahaspur, 4. Vikasnagar, 5. Kalsi, 6. Chakrata
8. Nainital **HQ:** Nainital	4,251	1. Nainital, 2. Haldwani 3. Dhari, 4. Koshya Kutauli 5. Ramnagar 6. Kala Dhungi 7. Betalghat 8. Lal Kuan	1. Okhalkanda, 2. Betalghat, 3. Ramgarh, 4. Bheemtal, 5. Dhari, 6. Kotabag, 7. Haldwani, 8. Ramnagar

Districts	Area (sq. km.)	Tehsils	Blocks
1	2	3	4
9. Pauri-Garhwal **HQ:** Pauri	5,329	1. Kotdwar, 2. Pauri 3. Thalisainn 4. Dhumakot 5. Shrinagar 6. Lansdowne 7. Yamakeshwar 8. Chaubattakhol 9. Satpuli 10. Chakisain	1. Khirsu, 2. Parakhet, 3. Pokhara, 4. Pauri, 5. Kaljikhal, 6. Yamakeshwar, 7. Beeronkhal, 8. Thalisainn, 9. Dwarikhal, 10. Dugadda, 11. Kote, 12. Nainidanda, 13. Lansdown, 14. Pawo, 15. Rikharikhal
10. Pithoragarh **HQ:** Pithoragarh	7,090	1. Dharchula 2. Munsyari 3. Pithoragarh 4. Deedeehat 5. Gangolihat 6. Berinag 7. Ganai Gangoli 8. Bangapani 9. Thal 10. Kanalichhina 11. Devalthal	1. Kanalichhina, 2. Deedeehat, 3. Berinag, 4. Dharchula, 5. Munsyari, 6. Gangolihat 7. Munakat, 8. Pithoragarh
11. Bageshwar **HQ:** Bageshwar	2,241	1. Bageshwar 2. Kapkote, 3. Garun 4. Kanda, 5. Kafligair 6. Dugnakuri	1. Garun, 2. Bageshwar, 3. Kapkote
12. Rudra Prayag **HQ:** Rudra Prayag	1,984	1. Rudra Prayag 2. Ukhimath 3. Jakholi 4. Basukedar	1. Ukhimath, 2. Augustmuni, 3. Jakholi
13. Haridwar **HQ:** Haridwar	2,360	1. Haridwar 2. Roorkee 3. Laxar 4. Bhagwanpur 5. Narsan	1. Roorkee, 2. Bhagwanpur, 3. Narsan, 4. Bahaderabad, 5. Laxar, 6. Khanpur

Note: The Uttarakhand government has issued a Government Order (GO) regarding creation of four new districts of Ranikhet, Didihaat, Kotdwar and Yamunotri. The GO, issued on December 8, 2011, however, did not mention the borders of the districts and their headquarters.

5   Economy

UTTARAKHAND economy mainly relies on tourism industry. Uttarakhand, being situated on the foothills of Himalayas, comprises of numerous hill stations which attract tourists from all across the globe thereby bringing money to the state. Apart from the hill stations, the wildlife have also been a major attraction for tourism as tourists come to visit the wildlife sanctuaries such as Corbett National Park and the famous Tiger Reserve.

The next most important contributor to the economy of Uttarakhand is the agricultural sector. As per the latest report net sown area is 74,1099 Hectare. Cereals, pulses, oilseeds, sugarcane and onion are the major crops growth here. Since majority of the population of Uttarakhand is occupied in agricultural sector, agriculture has to be among the top contributors of revenue in Uttarakhand economy.

Another important component on which the economy of Uttarakhand depends is its mineral resources. The state consists of large resources of minerals such as limestone rock phosphate, dolomite, magnesite, copper graphite, soap stone, gypsum and many others. Many of these minerals are exported out of India thereby fetching the Uttarakhand economy more revenue.

Uttarakhand economy also relies upon its small scale industries though they don't offer high revenues. The state has 55,545 small scale units and 995 Gramodhyog Units. The beautiful state also has 2,936 factories that are earning a very good profit.

Another component that is spreading its wing in Uttarakhand and is about to add lots of revenue to the Uttarakhand economy is the real estate. With more and more real estate agents eying on the picturesque locations of Uttarakhand, the day is not far away when real estate would be one of the major forces in determining the net flow of economy of Uttarakhand. A '**Money order economy**' also prevails in the region due to large-scale migration to the plains for jobs in the Armed Forces, Government or into the Private Sector.

The people of this State also go elsewhere in search of employment. They earn money and send to their native State. That is why the economy of this State is called 'Money Order Economy'. The main areas of employment for the people of Uttarakhand are–army, paramilitary, Government services, police, hotels and security *etc.*

The account of Uttarakhand was opened with total amount of rupees 2,192.08 crore on 9th November, 2000. Uttarakhand has got 2,600 crore rupees as a loan in the form of State heritage. According to Government information, the U.P. Government has loan of Rs. 780 thousand million. After the formation of Uttarakhand, the loan of 5.3% was transferred to Uttarakhand.

On the recommendation of Planning Commission, the State has been given special category on Ist April, 2001. Uttarakhand has become 11th State to get special facility. The other ten States to get special category of States are–Assam, Nagaland, Jammu & Kashmir, Himachal Pradesh, Manipur, Meghalaya, Tripura, Sikkim, Arunachal Pradesh and Mizoram.

The special category received States get special privileges and facilities. These States get Central Government help in the form of 90% as grant and 10% as loan whereas other States get 70% as grant and 30% as loan.

RESOURCES OF UTTARAKHAND

- **Water:** Ganga, Yamuna, Tonse, Kali, Gori, Ramganga flow from Uttarakhand.
- **Forest:** More than 2000 medicinal herbs are found in the forests of Uttarakhand.
- **Tourism:** Cultural, religious and adventurous tourism.
- **Minerals:** Magnesite, Granite, Graphite, Dolomite, Phosphorite, Gypsum, Copper, Barites and Chalk.
- **Product:** Flowers, fruits, fodder, mushroom, fishery, silk, wool, musk *etc.*
- **Per Head Income:** Per head income is a good measure to examine the development of economy growth rate. In year 2000-01, the per head income was estimated of Rs. 15,000. According to estimation of 2016-17 the per head income had reached to Rs. 1,61,102.

Economic Classification of Workers : 42% people of Uttarakhand are termed as workers and 58% are termed as non-workers. 87% of total workers are main workers and 13% are limited workers. 58.13% are farmers, 6.40% are agricultural labourers, 0.86% are engaged in cottage industries and remaining 34.61% are other workers.

INEQUALITIES IN THE UTTARAKHAND ECONOMY

Uttarakhand, the Himalayan state which borders along China, is the *sixth* richest state in India in terms of per capita income but those living in its hill districts benefit less from this development than those in the plains.

Consider this: The per capita income of Haridwar, a district in the plains that is 53 km from state capital Dehradun, is ₹ 122,172. But Uttarkashi, the northern-most Himalayan district, reports half that per capita income at ₹ 59,791, according to the 2014-15 Statistical Diary, Uttarakhand. This is close to the per capita income of Jharkhand which ranks among the 17th in the country.

The irony is that Uttarakhand was carved out of Uttar Pradesh (UP) in 2000 precisely so that exclusive attention could be given to the development of its remote hill districts. These had been left neglected by successive governments based in UP's capital Lucknow, around 600 km from Dehradun.

The mountain districts of Uttarakhand are still short of basic facilities, especially healthcare. There are no jobs to be had in these districts and this is leading to large-scale migration to the plains, leaving entire mountain villages uninhabited. And farming, which used to be the principal occupation in the hills, is crippled by small land holdings and a lack of government agri initiatives that neighbouring Himachal Pradesh sees in plenty.

"Uttarakhand was not founded for the development of Haridwar and Haldwani (cities in the plains) but for the development of the 16,000 plus villages in the hills of the state. But nothing is being done for them," said Anil Joshi, environmental activist and convenor of the Gaon Bachao Andolan (save the village movement), a campaign to tackle the state's migration issue.

At ₹ 122,804 Dehradun's own per capita income is closer to that of Haridwar. Though it is a hill district, it benefitted from being the state capital.

Uttarakhand's health infrastructure is facing a crisis, as IndiaSpend reported in February 2017-only 68% of its primary health centres that form the frontline of the public healthcare system work 24 x 7, as they are supposed to. The second-rung community health centres are short-staffed-they are 83% short of emergency specialists and have half the number of nurses needed.

Uttarakhand also suffers poor infant mortality rates (IMR), ranking 18th among 29 states, according to an Observer Research Foundation analysis. But the hill districts of Rudraprayag, Pithoragarh and Almora record fewer infant deaths despite their inaccessible terrain. It is the well-developed pilgrim district of Haridwar that reports the worst figure of 70 deaths per 1,000 infants (2012-13), the same as conflict-ridden Congo. Haridwar also represents a high rate of stunting-low weight for height 52% in children under five, compared to Pithorgarh's 22%.

Himachal Pradesh too has a problem accessing hilly districts but it is doing much better than Uttarakhand on the healthcare front as this comparative report of the two states for 2014-15 shows. Himachal Pradesh has 141 beds per 100,000 people compared to 86 beds in Uttarakhand-which has 47% more population (10 million) than the former (6.8 million). Himachal Pradesh has nearly double the primary health centres (500) Uttarakhand does (258). And its community health centres (78) outnumber those in Uttarakhand (59).

1,048 Villages Emptied out Completely in the Hills

People living in the mountains have always migrated to cities in the plains in search of white-collar jobs. But they would leave their families, or a part of it, behind. Now migrations to the plains involve entire families moving from the hills to the plains, either within Uttarakhand or to other parts of the country.

While hill districts saw a decadal population growth of 12.75%, the plains recorded almost 32%. This is a sure sign of large scale migration of entire families from the hills.

There are 1,048 villages in the state that are uninhabited-"ghost villages", according to Census 2011. Here migration has emptied out entire villages.

There has been a negative decadal growth observed in the districts of Almora (-1.28%) and Pauri Garhwal (-1.41%). The population in both districts together fell by 17,868 persons between 2001 and 2011.

In 2015, the National Institute for Rural Development and Panchayat Raj conducted a survey of 217 households in Almora and Pauri Garhwal to understand the dynamics of migration and its impact on the village economy. They found the following: 88% of households reported having at least one person migrating for a job; 86% of those who had migrated were men, 51% of them were between 30-49 years. Also, 73% of them reported migrating for durations between six and 12 months.

The top reason for migration was employment—47% of migrants cited the lack of job opportunities in their home districts. And 18% said they migrated anticipating better jobs in cities while 17% said they had landed jobs or were being transferred out by their existing employers.

"The attraction to cities arising due to hardships of village life in hills such as poor transport connectivity, lack of water, inadequate medical facilities, poor educational facilities and inaccessible markets have (sic) further accelerated the process of migration of youth," said the report.

Agriculture Growth Slows to 4%

There has been slowing down of growth in agriculture and allied activities in Uttarakhand. Its annual, average growth stood at 4% between 2010 and 2015 compared to Himachal Pradesh's 9% in the same period.

"Himachal Pradesh earns more than ₹ 15,000 crore every year from horticulture and agriculture because of its government policies. The Uttarakhand government never focussed on developing agriculture and that is why there is this deep decline".

Also, smaller land holdings give smaller returns on investment and 73% of all farmers in the state are marginal, with less than 1 hectare of land according to the state statistical diary.

With migrants abandoning their land to the elements, vacated farmlands are attracting wild animals from surrounding forests and this is leading to animal-human conflicts. Even though a notification passed in February 2016 allows the culling of wild boars, the implementation of the notification has been poor.

"An upwards altitudinal shift in cropping has been reported in cash crops like apple, rajma, potato and carrot. Some projections speculate on an increase of night time temperature (Dimri and Dash, 2011) which may not only lead to decrease in production of some crops such as rice, but also reduce the winter killing of pests, hereby decreasing crop yields," said 2015: Climate Change in Uttarakhand, a report by the Centre for Ecology, Development and Research.

There has also a drop in annual rainfall in the region that has impacted the state's dominantly rain-dependent farming. Most of the old water sources are drying up, agriculture is becoming very challenging.

An analysis of temperature and rainfall data over 100 years shows a decline in rainfall that grew steeper after 1970s. "Although the average reduction rate in annual total rainfall has been insignificant, yet it may put great stress on the water resources of the region. The rainfall declining trend (sic) is not the same all over the state," noted Changing Climate of Uttarakhand, a paper published in 2014 in the journal Geology and Geosciences.

State Finances

THE appointment of a state finance commission is provided for under Articles 243 I and 243 Y of the Constitution, whereby in every five year, the state is required to constitute such a commission. The first State Finance Commission of Uttarakhand was constituted on 31st March 2001. Its recommendations were applicable from 1 April 2001 to 31 March 2006. The Second State Finance Commission was constituted on 30 April 2005, which submitted its report on 6 June 2006. Its recommendations were applicable from 1 April 2006 to 31 March 2011. The Third State Finance Commission was constituted on 2nd December 2009 with Shri I. K. Pandey as Chairman. Its recommendations are to apply from 1 April 2011 to 31 March 2016.

The main tasks of the state finance commissions are:

1. Distribution between the state and panchayats/municipalities of the net proceeds of the taxes, duties, tolls and fees liveable by the state.
2. Determination of the taxes, duties, tolls and fees which may be assigned as, or appropriated by, panchayats/municipalities
3. Grants-in-aid to panchayats/municipalities from the Consolidated Fund of the State
4. Measures needed to improve the financial position of panchayats/municipalities
5. Any other matter referred to the Finance Commission by the governor in the interest of sound finance of panchayats/municipalities.

LOCAL BODIES IN UTTARAKHAND: MAIN FEATURES

The revenue collections in a particular region are impacted by the level of economic activity as measured by the gross domestic product. This impacts the tax base as well as the tax paying capacity of the citizens. Although at the state level Uttarakhand has performed well, there are wide inter-district variations in terms of economic performance within the state. This can be seen from Table.

District Domestic Product of Uttarakhand (2008-09 Advance Estimates)

S.No.	District	At Constant Prices (1999-2000)		At Current prices	
		GDDP	Per Capita in ₹	GDDP	Per Capita in ₹
1.	Uttarkashi	65,361	19,598	96,136	28,826
2.	Chamoli	1,12,775	26,936	1,58,560	37,871
3.	Rudraprayag	48,608	18,905	70,744	27,515
4.	Tehri Garhwal	1,79,385	26,239	2,61,787	38,292
5.	Dehradun	5,01,701	34,614	7,27,215	50,172
6.	Garhwal	1,81,292	23,006	2,54,912	32,348
7.	Pithoragarh	1,20,273	23,014	1,71,228	32,764
8.	Bageshwar	47,893	16,983	72,653	25,762
9.	Almora	1,66,152	23,308	2,33,608	32,771
10.	Champawat	55,224	21,756	80,100	31,555
11.	Nainital	2,78,787	32,325	4,07,192	47,213
12.	Udham Singh Nagar	3,64,327	26,082	5,39,839	38,647
13.	Haridwar	6,29,780	38,495	9,41,952	57,576
	Total	**27,51,558**	**28,671**	**40,15,926**	**41,846**

Source: Report of the Third State Finance Commission of Uttarakhand, 2011-16

Per capita DDP at current prices varies between ₹ 25,762 (Bageshwar) and ₹ 38,292 (Tehri Garhwal) among hill districts. Amongst plain districts the per capita income varies between ₹ 38,647 (U.S. Nagar) to ₹ 57,576 (Haridwar). Only Nainital despite being a hilly region had a per capita DDP of ₹ 47,213. Industrial and concomitantly services growth has occurred predominantly in the districts of Udham Singh Nagar, Dehradun and Haridwar.

The structure of decentralised governance in Uttarakhand is similar to other states. The rural governance system consists of three tiers of Panchayati Raj institutions (PRIs) – gram panchayats at the village level, kshetra panchayats at the level of development block and zilla panchayats at the district level. Urban Local bodies are similarly divided into Nagar Nigams, Nagar Palika Parishads and Nagar Panchayats. Nagar Panchayats represent places that are in transition from a rural status to an urban status.

Both the systems face several issues that the Third State Finance Commission highlights in its report.

PANCHAYATI RAJ INSTITUTIONS (PRIS)

In 2010, there were 7,541 gram panchayats covering 15,761 villages, 95 kshetra panchayats and 13 zila panchayats. Key characteristics of the PRI system in Uttarakhand are as follows:

1. **Large number of Gram Panchayats:** After the formation of the new state, the government tried to rationalise the number of gram Panchayats to prevent the proliferation of small rural bodies. It fixed the minimum and maximum population for a gram panchayat at 300 and 1,000 in the hilly parts and at 1,000 and 5,000 for the plains respectively. However, its efforts have been unsuccessful so far. More than 812 gram panchayats still exist with a population of less than 300. The total number of panchayats too increased from 7055 in 2002 to 7541 in 2010.

2. **Overlapping functions:** The UP Zila Panchayat and Kshetra Panchayat Act, 1961 assigns almost similar functions to Zila Panchayats and Kshetra Panchayats. Similarly the U.P. Panchayat Raj Act, 1947 assigns similar functions to the Gram Panchayats. This has resulted in a non-hierarchical structure of the PRIs with independent functioning of each level.

3. **Large variation in Size of Zila Panchayats:** In terms of population size, zila panchayats vary from a minimum of 2 lakhs (approx.) in Champawat to a maximum of 10 lakhs (approx.) in Haridwar. In terms of area too, the zila panchayat size varies from a low of 1,000 sq. kms in Champawat to 8,000 sq kms in Uttarkashi.

An important deficiency that underlines the relatively inadequate performance of local bodies both rural and urban pertains to inadequate capacities of these bodies interms of human resources as well as physical infrastructure. In the case of urban local bodies, such capacities are needed not only to meet the regular responsibilities but also additional programmes like JNNURM, IDSMT, BSUP and IHSDP, which require sophisticated skills and capacities. The Third State Finance Commission has also observed that the 63 ULBs in Uttarakhand are at present extremely deficient in terms of these capacities, both in terms of human resources and infrastructure that could facilitate more effective functioning through e-governance and other capacity enhancing initiatives.

These ULBs in the state are also saddled with certain major constraints on account of their peculiar situation. They are required to cater for a large non-minimal revenue paying floating population on account of the fact that a large number of them are pilgrim destinations or on the Yatra route. Many others are important tourist destinations. While the level of economic activity and paying capacity is low, given their hill nature, the responsibilities on this account are onerous.

DEVOLUTION OF FUNDS TO LOCAL BODIES

RURAL LOCAL BODIES

The Third State Finance Commission determined the devolution scheme of funds for PRIs (50% of the total amount) for the years 2011-15 as given in Table.

Shares of Various Categories of Panchayati Raj Institutions:

S.No.	Category of PRI	Number of respective PRIs in the state	Weightage
1	Gram Panchayats	7541	50%
2	Kshetra Panchayats	95	20%
3	Zila Panchayats	13	30%

Source: *Report of the Third State Finance Commission, Uttarakhand*

The maximum weight has been given to the Gram Panchayats by the Commission. The share of Kshetra Panchayats and Zila Panchayats was determined as 30% and 20% respectively by the Second State Finance Commission. However, the Third State Finance Commission devolved a greater percentage of funds to the Zila Panchayats keeping in mind that Kshetra Panchayats have neither any independent functions, functionaries, funds or assets of their own.

Devolution to the Zila Panchayats and Kshetra Panchayats was determined on the basis of the common criteria of population, area and remoteness. Tax effort was used as an additional criterion for Zila Panchayat, while the number of gram panchayats was used as a criterion for Kshetra Panchayats. Table gives details of the devolution criteria used within each category of PRI.

Weightage Scheme for Inter-se Distribution of the devolution within each category of PRI:

(Percent)

Criteria	Zila Panchayats	Kshetra Panchayats	Gram Panchayats (GPs)
Population	50	60	80
Area	20	15	20
Remoteness	15	15	
Tax Effort	15		
No. of GPs		10	

Source: *Report of the Third State Finance Commission, Uttarakhand*

Due to unavailability of data, only two factors namely population and area have been considered to devolve funds amongst gram panchayats. To overcome the problem of inadequate funding determined by the formula, the floor population was fixed at 300 for gram panchayats having population lesser than this threshold. This was in accordance with the minimum population size prescribed for Gram Panchayats in the hilly parts of the state under the Uttarakhand amendment to the U.P. Panchayat Raj Act, 1947.

URBAN LOCAL BODIES

Uttarakhand has a total of 72 municipal bodies consisting of one old Nagar Nigam (Dehradun) and five recently notified Nagar Nigams (Haridwar, Haldwani, Kashipur, Rudrapur and Roorkee), 28 Nagar Palika Parishads and 35 elected Nagar Panchayats and 3 non-elected Nagar Panchayats, 12 Census Towns and two Industrial Townships. The U.P. Municipal Corporation Act, 1959 governs all municipal corporations while the U.P. Municipalities Act, 1916 is applicable to the Nagar Palika Parishads and Nagar Panchayats.

The key issues facing the ULBs in Uttarakhand are as follows:

1. **Urban degradation:** Rapid urbanisation has led to additional pressure on urban infrastructure such as roads, slums, sewage etc. This has resulted in increased pollution, environmental degradation, filth and squalor in the cities of Dehradun, Haldwani, Haridwar, Roorkee and Kashipur among others.

2. **Wide Variation in Population:** The classification of urban bodies in the state exhibits wide variation in its population covered. For example, excluding the 6 Nagar Nigams, the most populated Nagar Palika Parishad (Rishikesh) has more than 32 times the population of the least populated one (Dogadda). Similarly, the most populated Nagar Panchayat (Laksar) has more than 10 times the population of the least populated pachayat (Nandprayag). The population of Laksar itself is more than that of 11 Nagar Palika Parishads. The population of census towns too ranges from 3,739 (Dharchula Dehat) to 24,921 (Raipur). Hence, there is an urgent need to reclassify the various levels of governance systems to make them more symmetric in terms of population coverage. The Third State Finance Commission of Uttarakhand proposes that the 2011 census could be used as the basis for such a reclassification.

7 | Industries

IN recent years, Uttarakhand has emerged as one of the most attractive industrial destinations in India. The government is encouraging private participation in all industrial activities and as a result big players such as HLL and Dabur have set up units in the state. The New Industrial Policy announced in 2003 by the state government puts in place the regulatory framework for Uttarakhand's industrialisation. The New Industrial Policy indicates that private resources may be tapped while promoting integrated Industrial Estates in Uttarakhand.

INDUSTRIAL POLICY - 2008

The existing Industrial Policy was framed in the back-drop of potentialities and expectations of the newly created State of Uttarakhand. The policy focused on the sectors where Uttarakhand has inherent advantages *e.g.,* Tourism, Floriculture, Agro and Food processing, Handloom, Khadi and Village Industries etc.

The aim is to provide a comprehensive framework to enable a facilitating, investor friendly environment for ensuring rapid and sustainable industrial development in Uttarakhand and, through this, to generate additional employment opportunities and to bring about a significant increase in the State Domestic Product and eventual widening of the resource base of the State. This will be termed as the New Industrial Policy 2008.

VISION

- To create high quality world class infrastructure facilities in the State and enhance, in particular, connectivity to the National Capital Region (NCR) and other leading markets.

- To provide single window facilitation in the State to expedite project clearances and provide an investor friendly climate.

- To provide and facilitate expeditious land availability for setting Industrial ventures and Infrastructure projects.

- To promote and encourage private sector participation in the development and management of infrastructure projects such as Industrial Estates/ Areas, Growth Centers, IIDCs, Special Economic and Commodity Zones and Parks, Theme Parks, Tourism infrastructure, development of new tourist destinations, Airports/Helipads/Airstrips, Roads, generation, transmission and distribution of power, and projects in the area of Horticulture, Floriculture, Bio-technology etc.

- To provide assured, good quality, uninterrupted and affordable power for industries.

- To simplify and rationalize labour laws and procedures in tune with the current day requirements, while ensuring that the workers get their due share in the economic prosperity of the State.

- To promote, in particular, Small scale, Cottage and Khadi and Village Industries and Handicrafts Silk and Handloom sectors, assist them in modernization and technological up-gradation and provide the necessary common facilities and backward and forward linkages, including product design and marketing support so as to make them globally competitive and remunerative.

- To address problems of sickness and incipient sickness in Industry, particularly SSIs and facilitate required restructuring and rehabilitation, etc. in coordination with the Banks and financial institutions.

TYPES OF INDUSTRIES

Industries of Uttarakhand form the basis of the economic set up of Uttarakhand. The State Industrial Corporation of Uttarakhand has developed seven industrial estates; and thus it is helping the industries of Uttarakhand to develop further.

Industries in the perspective of today's world plays a large role in the consolidating the socio-economic rubric of a state. Previously, agriculture used to the basis of the economic set up, but after the Industrial Revolution, agriculture has taken a back-seat.

In this respect, industries in Uttarakhand are the means of resurgence in the economy of Uttarakhand. In fact, it is the industries that is helping the government of Uttarakhand to compete with the other States.

Uttarakhand, nestled in the foothills of the Himalayas, houses a lot of mineral resources which largely contribute towards the industrial development of the State.

SOME OF THE MAJOR INDUSTRIES IN UTTARAKHAND ARE:

- Electrical Engineering
- Cement plants
- Pharmaceuticals
- Textile
- Arms and Ammunition
- Food Processing *etc.*

It is noteworthy that despite having a rugged terrain the industries of Uttarakhand have shown a tremendous development. Some of the factors that is supposed to have supported the growth of industries in this area are:

- easy availability of raw materials
- transport facility
- availability of cheap labor
- enterprising Government *etc.*

According to the statistics, there are 55,545 small-scale industries and 995 Khadi Udhyog/Gramodhyog Units in Uttarakhand. Moreover, there are as many as 2936 big industries providing employment to over 3,86,654 persons in Uttarakhand. But it is noteworthy that most of the industries are forest based industries. Thus, it can be said that the industries play a significant role in the economy of Uttarakhand.

AGRO AND FOOD PROCESSING INDUSTRIES

The state government provides assistance in establishing small and medium size agro parks, food parks *etc.*, which in turn are expected to provide common infrastructure facilities for storage, processing, grading and marketing.

Four Agri Export Zones (AEZs) have already been declared under the AEZ scheme of Government of India for leechi, horticulture, herbs, medicinal plants and basmati rice.

Uttarakhand has been included in difficult area category by the Ministry of Food Processing Industry (MFPI) and hence units being set up in Uttarakhand will be eligible for higher incentives under the scheme of MFPI.

The state government is also providing matching subsidy for projects under various schemes of Agricultural and Processed Food Products Export Development Authority (APEDA), National Horticulture Board (NHB), Ministry of Food Processing Industry (MFPI) and the Natural Medicinal Plant Board (NMPB) subject to a maximum limit of ₹ 20 lakhs.

BIOTECHNOLOGY

Biotechnology (BT) is poised to make significant contributions in agriculture, human and animal health care, environment management and process **industries**. Rare species of plants and animals found in the state, add to its natural advantage in this sector. In this context, a MOU has already been signed between Rabo India Finance Company, Infrastructure Development Finance Company and the G.B. Pant University of Agriculture and Technology in order to forge strategic cooperation to jointly pursue initiatives in the sphere of research in food and agriculture sectors. A high level Biotechnology Board is also being set up under the Chairmanship of the Hon'ble Chief Minister.

The proposed strategy of the state with respect to the biotechnology sector is:

- Units coming up in this sector, including the R&D units in this field, shall be accorded industry status and the provisions made for the IT sector shall be made applicable to this sector as well.

- Establish an internationally competitive business infrastructure and environment for the biotechnology industry in the state.

- Develop Uttarakhand as a centre of excellence in biotechnology by providing necessary education and training facilities for the creation of a large pool of multi-skilled, technically competent manpower and organizations for state of the art biotechnology research in the state.

- A biotechnology park will be developed near Pantnagar to achieve the vision of the government. The proposed Biotechnology Park will integrate resources and provide amongst others, a focused institutional set up for accelerated commercial growth of Biotechnology and Bio-Informatics.

INFORMATION AND COMMUNICATION TECHNOLOGY

The state is naturally endowed and has all prerequisites for developing as a preferred destination for IT & ITes along with hardware production. IT & ITes have been accorded the status of Industry. Several initiatives have been taken to promote IT ITes industry in Uttarakhand. Uttarakhand offers high-speed connectivity with the establishment of an STPI earth station at Dehradun and proposed earth stations at other locations. Facilities by BSNL and Reliance are also available in the state. A dedicated IT park is already coming up in Dehradun and others are in the pipeline. Also, stamp duty concessions are proposed for units located in IT parks.

FOREST PRODUCTS-HERBS AND SPICES

Since a significant part of the state is under the forest cover (almost 45.32 per cent), there exists excellent potential for the development of forest resources based industries. In addition, there is ample scope to develop industries based on forest and agro wastes such as lantana, pine needles and plant & vegetative fibers.

Uttarakhand is also a storehouse for a rich variety of herbs, medicinal and aromatic plant species. With a view to utilize these resources, a medicinal and aromatic plants export zone has been set up covering seven districts of Uttarakhand and specialized herbal parks are in the offing.

TOURISM

Tourism industry has been accorded the status of a thrust sector in the state and the state government has set up statutory Uttarakhand Tourism Board as an apex body for development of tourism in the state. Several areas of Uttarakhand are already established as centres of pilgrimage tourism. Huge investment potential exists in the tourism sector including:

- Development of facilities for providing spiritual lessons, reiki, and other rejuvenating courses.
- Eco-tourism hotels, spa, resorts, amusement parks and ropeways.
- Winter sports at places such as Auly, which have the requisite terrain for the purpose.
- Adventure tourism.

A detailed and separate tourism policy has also been formulated under which a multitude of incentives have been provided to boost the industry:

- New tourism units will be allowed rebate/deferment facility in respect of luxury tax for a period of five years from the date of commencement.
- New ropeways installed in the state will be exempt from payment of entertainment tax for a period of five years from the date of commencement.
- New amusement parks set up will be exempt from entertainment tax for a period of five years from the date of becoming fully operational.

UDYOG MITRA

At the State level, Udyog Mitra has been setup under the Chairmanship of Hon'ble Chief Minister as an apex interactive, policy and problem redressal body with the concerned Ministers, Government officials, Banks, FIs and representatives from the Industrial Associations as its members.

The District level Udyog Mitra has been setup under the Chairmanship of District Magistrate for the above purpose. Its membership includes the district level officials of the various departments, Banks, FIs and representatives of Industrial associations.

HANDICRAFTS

Uttarakhand's potential for traditional Handicraft items, will be tapped by aggressive support in the area of Marketing, Design upgradation and provision of adequate backward and forward linkages. Under Baba Saheb Ambedkar Hast Shilp Vikas Yojna and other centrally sponsored schemes, a package of support to artisans and handicraft artisans will be provided which include basic inputs and infrastructure support like diagnostic survey and project plan, mobilization of artisans, training, design development, new techniques, packing, common facility centre, marketing events, exhibitions, emporiums and publicity.

The traditional handicrafts like woollen carpet, wood carving, *ringal* crafts and copper crafts, etc shall be encouraged through various initiatives like:-

- Training by Master Craftsmen will be organised *in situ* and these locations will be developed as "Shilp Grams".
- Action will be taken to promote and develop Handicraft products as souvenir items, and facilitation of their marketing in Tourist and Commercial Centres within and outside the State.
- Efforts will be made to promote export of these items by organizing fairs, development of showrooms with private participation, and support in the area of publicity.
- An Urban Haat is being developed in Dehradun and Rural Handicrafts Centres (Gramin Shilp Kendras) are being developed in the other districts for the display and marketing of Handicraft products.
- A Crafts Design Center is also proposed to be developed in district Nainital with a view to develop new designs and products in line with the market demand.
- In order to encourage diamond cutting & polishing and gem industry, a Gem and Jewellery Park is proposed to be established in the State.

HANDLOOMS

This Industry is of vital importance for employment generation in rural areas.

- Under the Deen Dayal Hathkargha Protsahan Yojna action will be taken to benefit Cooperative Societies or registered groups of Handloom weavers. Members of these groups would be imparted training as well as be provided with modern looms and designs.
- Action will be taken for facilitating the marketing of their products by setting up showrooms in public-private partnership and motivating them to export their produce.

- Establishment, expansion and modernization of Design Centres will also be undertaken.

- The State Government proposes to develop Integrated Handloom Complexes where facilities for dyeing, carding, development of designs, etc. will be provided.

- Silk and silk products have been declared as thrust industries. Keeping in view the availability of high quality of silk in the State, silk production and its allied activities will be encouraged and steps will be taken to modernise the existing industries as well as to promote the measures for value addition.

INDUSTRIAL AREAS / ESTATES / PARKS

Integrated Industrial Estate Haridwar: Integrated Industrial Estate Haridwar (Uttarakhand)–Located just 3 Km from Delhi-Haridwar National Highway. 225 Km from National Capital Delhi and 52 Km from State Capital Dehradun.

Integrated Industrial Estate Pantnagar: Located at National Highway no. NH-87. 235 Km from National Capital Delhi and 300 Km from State Capital Dehradun.

Pharma City Selaqui Industrial Area Dehradun: Pharma City Selaqui Industrial Area Dehradun (Uttarakhand) - Located 25 Km from Dehradun. 225 Km from National Capital Delhi.

Information Technology Park Dehradun: Information Technology Park at Dehradun–(SIDCUL), as the nodal agency to promote the development of industrialization in the State of Uttarakhand, has prioritized the establishment of International Quality–IT infrastructure in the state.

Integrated Industrial Estate Sitarganj: State administration embarked on a comprehensive programme of driving industrial growth in the state. In line with the above vision of economic development of Uttarakhand, state of the art Integrated Industrial Estate (IIE) is envisaged at Sitarganj in Udham Singh Nagar district by State Industrial Development Corporation of Uttarakhand Limited (SIDCUL).

Mineral Resources

MINERAL resources of Uttarakhand plays a significant role in the economy of Uttarakhand. Although, the mineral resources of Uttarakhand are not as varied as that of Jharkhand or Odisha; yet mineral resources at Uttarakhand largely contribute towards the economic well being of the state.

The Chamoli district of Uttarakhand is especially famous for housing a number of mineral resources in Uttarakhand. The northern division of the district consist entirely of medium to high grade metamorphic rocks, which also contains bands of volcanic rocks in some areas; the southern division contains sedimentary and low-grade metamorphic rocks, with bands of volcanic rocks in some regions.

Although much is not known about the geology of the first division of Chamoli, yet the mineral resources contain rocks such as quartzite, marble, and various types of schist and gneiss. The southern division contains rocks such as gneiss, limestone, phyllites, quartzite, sericite-biotite schist and slate.

Some of the important minerals that form a major part of the mineral resources of Uttarakhand are:

- Asbestos
- Copper
- Graphite
- Lead
- Building Stone
- Magnestic
- Iron
- Gold
- Slate
- Sulphur, and
- Soapstone or Steatite
- Graphite
- Gypsum
- Limestone
- Bitumen

Beside these major mineral resources, some of the other mineral resources of Uttarakhand also play a major role in enhancing the economy of Uttarakhand. Some of those mineral resources are:

- Antimony
- Lignite or Brown Marble
- Silver, *etc.*
- Arsenic
- Mica

Thus, as it is evident, the mineral resources in Uttarakhand is found in abundant. In fact, it is through these mineral resources that Uttarakhand is striding forward in this competitive world.

BRIEF DESCRIPTION OF MINERALS

Magnesite : The biggest magnesite store of India is present in Kumaon region of Uttarakhand. It is also found in abundance in Chamoli district of Garhwal region. Magnesite is present mostly in Jhirauli, Devaldhar, Tapovan, Pokhari, Belakuchi, Joshimath, Mandakini Valley, Pinder Valley *etc.* places. The work for extracting Magnesite is going on at Jhirauli in Almora district and at Chandak in Pithoragarh districts. The first furnace of Magnesite Project started functioning on 26th October, 1977 which is established at the cost of Rs. one crore 73 lakh at Chandak. It is the second project of its kind in hilly region after Jhirauli.

Magnesite has a large utility. It is used on a large scale in the big furnaces of iron, steel and cement factories as heat-proof. Various types of mix-metals are manufactured by mixing it with Aluminium, Copper, Nickel, Zink and other metals. It is also used in purifying oil and manufacturing acid.

Chalk : Magnesite and Chalk are generally found together because these have genetic relation. Chalk is found in hilly areas of Jakhera, Aagar-Girichhina, Lohar Valley, Muwani, Devasthal, Kanda, Rai-Aagar, Tarosi and Huyena regions of Chamoli Tehsil. There are repositories of Chalk in Mandakini Valley and Pinder Valley.

Chalk is used in making statues, decorating things, pesticides, fertilizers, craft-paper, electric appliances, and greasy powders.

Lime-Stone and Marble : Lime-stone is found in Kumaon and Garhwal. It is present in abundance at ookhimath Tehsil, Alakhnanda Valley, in the middle of Pinder and Lohaba Strip, adjoining areas of Tehri and Dehradun, near Neelkanth and east of Rishikesh. It is also found on large scale at Gangolihat of Pithoragarh district and in Nainital and Almora districts. Marble is found in Alakhnanda Valley of Chamoli Tehsil and Virahi Ganga Valley. Nearabout 4 million tons marble is found near Mussourie.

Rock Phosphate : The digging of rock phosphate in Mussourie (Dehradun) and Tehri-Garhwal is being done by 'Pyrites Phosphates & Chemical Limited'. There are big repositories of rock phosphate at Durmala, Kimoi, Masarana, Mal Devata and Chamasari. Its new areas are found recently in Nainital district. This mineral is used in fertilizer industries and for the treatment of acidic soil.

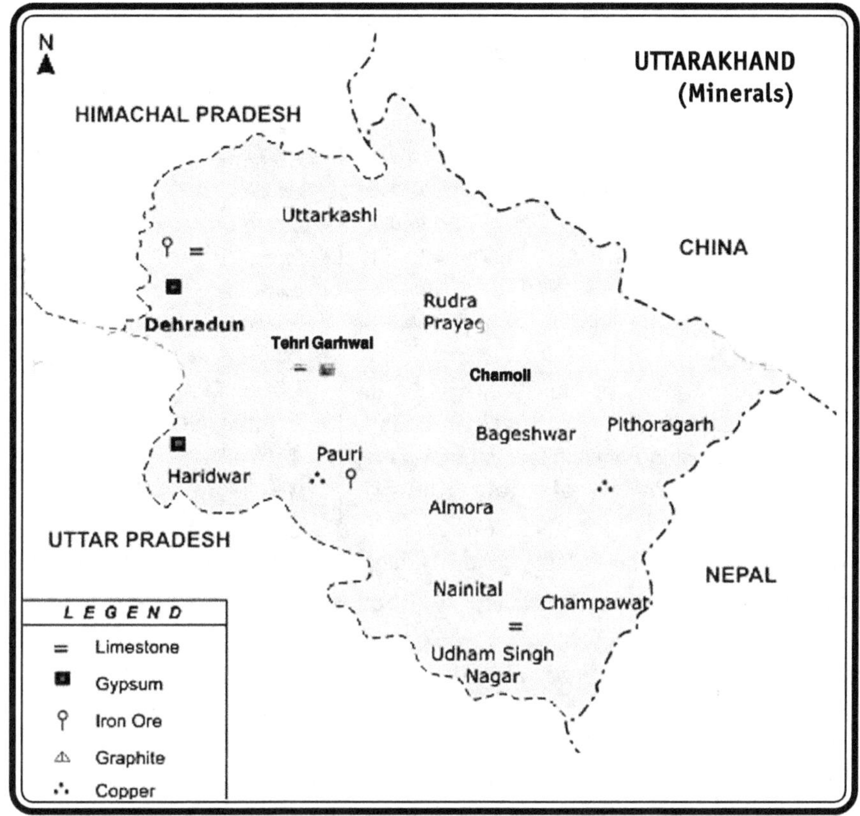

Gold: It is achieved from the sands of Sharda and Ramganga rivers. It is a costly metal. It is achieved in form of particles in the sands of Pindar of Alakhnanda and Sone rivers. Gold is used in making medicines, electro-plating, photography, to polish the glass-bangles and making ornaments.

Iron: It is found at Ramgarh, Kaladungi of Nainital district, Chandpur Patti of Garhwal, Rajbaguna, Kaliphat, Dudhatoli, Chopra, Lohagaon, Dasoli *etc.*

Coal: Its digging work is being done in Kumaon and Garhwal regions of Uttarakhand. The digging of coal is being done in Kumaon and Garhwal regions under the direction of Indian Geological Survey Department.

Stone and Slab: In ancient time, the stone used in the roofs of houses of hilly region–represents that it is found everywhere in Uttarakhand. In Almora district, good quality of slabs are found. These are used for the construction of roofs, courtyards, drains, roads *etc.*

Lead: It is found at Chandak, Devalgarh, Ralam and Bhainskhal of Pithoragarh district, Ranei of Almora district, Nagpur region of Garhwal, Kuma-Burela and Mughaul in Tonse river valley of Dehradun district. Some lead is also found in Almora district (Chainapani and Bilaun region). It is used in transport appliances and fertilizers. It is heavy and elastic metal.

Gypsum: It is found near Khiyarkuli and Bhata villages in Dehradun district of Uttarakhand, near Dhapila village of Nainital district, Kharari valley of Garhwal district, Kharari, Laxmanjhula, Gudhthani regions.

- **Lime stone:** Dehradun (Chakrata), Garhwal (Lensdown), Tehri, Pithoragarh
- **Dolomite:** Tehri and Dehradun
- **Magnetite:** Almora, Pithoragarh, Chamoli
- **Copper:** Chamoli, Almora, Nainital
- **Gypsum:** Garhwal, Dehradun, Nainital
- **Marble:** Dehradun and Tihri Garhwal
- **Phosphorite:** Tehri and Rajgewan
- **Iron Ore:** Garhwal, Almora and Nainital
- **Asbestos:** Garhwal and Almora
- **Rock phosphates:** Kumaon, Nainital, Tehri, Mussourie
- **Lead:** Kumayun, Dehradun
- **Silver:** Almora

Sulphur: It is found near Sutaul village 50 km east of Nandprayag in Uttarakhand.

Uranium: Indication for its availability is found in Tehri-Garhwal region of Uttarakhand.

Talc: It is found in Pithoragarh and Almora districts of Uttarakhand. It is very soft mineral. It is used in making talcum powder, paints, soap, pesticide powder, textile and paper *etc.*

Silver: It is found in Almora district in a small quantity.

Asbestos: It is found in Garhwal (Ookhimath and Kandhera) and Almora districts of Uttarakhand. It is chiefly used in cement manufacturing and electric appliances. Asbestos has capacity to bear high heat-stroke and it does not react too much in chemical reaction. Due to this, it is used in industrial area on a large scale. The mixture of lime and magnesium is found in it.

9 | Agriculture, Horticulture & Fishing

A PART from tourism, the economy of the state is predominantly agrarian. 90 per cent of the working population is directly engaged in agriculture. Doon Valley, Nainital district, Udham Singh Nagar and Haridwar districts produce large quantities of food grains. The state has immense potential for the development of horticulture crops-apple, orange, malta, pear, grapes

peach, plum appricot, litchi, mango, guava *etc.* are widely produced fruits.

Other important occupations include forestry, sheep rearing and livestock farming and household or cottage industries. A less developed state of the non- primary sectors result in high dependency on agriculture and uneconomic cultivation of crops together with the environmental limits create not only a condition of deficit but also a 'disguised' unemployment.

Mountain, and Himalayan agriculture specifically, deviates substantially from the kinds practiced in less precipitous altitudes. Hill farmers the world over have adapted to the difficult geography, and the terrain has likewise influenced cultural modes in mountain societies. Patterns of land ownership, subsistence vs. surplus production, and level of market penetration have also been decisively affected.

Agriculture takes place in the river valleys of Uttarakhand (a meagre 10-15% of the total land area). Over time, several slops have been shaped into field terraces, a common trend in mountain agriculture everywhere. The Uttarakhand farmers have also developed advanced manure, crop rotation, and inter-cropping practices. Most land along the slopes remains unirrigated. Three tyeps of agriculture are traced to these river valleys adapting to the type of land:

- **Katil** (forest edge land)
  Hoe cultivation, rotation of 3 crops in 5 years
  Important crops: millets, amaranth

- **Upraon** (hillside land)
  Always terraced, but unirrigated
  Important crops: mandua, jhangora, chaulai
- **Talaon** (valley bottom land)
  Paddy cultivation, low-lying, irrigated, double cropped
  Important crops: wheat, rice, sugarcane, *etc.*

Ecological sub-region	*Altitude (m)*	*Chief Crops*
Lower Dun, Terai	300-600	wheat, rice, sugarcane
Upper Dun, Bhabar, lower Shivaliks	600-1,200	wheat, rice, mandua, jhangora, chaulai, maize
Middle Garhwal-Kumaon	1,200-1,800	wheat, rice, mandua, jhangora, "cheena", potato, barley
Upper Garhwal-Kumaon	1,800-2,400	wheat, barley, potato, chaulai, cheena, "phaphra"
Cold Zone	2,400-3,600	wheat, barley, potato, phaphra, chaulai, "kauni", "ogal"

Different pulses are inter-cropped during the two harvest periods-

- early winter after the rainy season (millet)
- midsummer before the hot dry season (barley-wheat)

Dry and wet rice, taro, pumpkins, beans, corn, ginger, chili, cucumbers, leafy vegetables and tobacco are also cultivated. Potatoes have developed into a principal cash crop growing in areas unpropitious for other plants.

Agriculture comprises an important factor contributing to the economy of Uttarakhand.

Conventional Himalayan agriculture is being destroyed by market stresses, introducing both economic and cultural modifications in Uttarakhand. Ancient self-sufficiency has been replaced by dependency on imports from the plains, with their pesticide or chemical fertilizer-enhanced products. Cultural domination from the plains also poses a threat to the usual foods as an increasing preference for mill-polished rice is triumphing over mountain crops. Activists in the hills have responded with a 'Save the Seeds' campaign and are generating awareness about the necessity for biodiversity in agriculture.

NET AND GROSS IRRIGATED AREA IN 2013-14 IN HECTARES

1.	Canals	79463
2.	Tube Wells	209772
3.	Other Wells	15944
4.	Tanks/Ponds	57
5.	Other Sources	22868
6.	Net Irrigated Area (NIA)	328104
7.	Gross Irrigated Area (GIA)	544084

IRRIGATIONAL INFRASTRUCTURE IN 2014-15

1.	Length of Canals	12215 km
2.	Length of Lift Canals	278 km
3.	Tube Wells (State)	1353 No.
4.	Pump Sets (Boring/Free Boaring)	55456 No.
5.	Hauj	36761 No.
6.	Gool	29785 km
7.	Hydrum	1475 No.
8.	C.C.A. Under State Canal	3.437 Lakh Hectare
9.	Revenue Collection by Irrigation	₹ 244.40 Lakh

LAND DISTRIBUTION

The pattern of land ownership is unlike that found in the rest of India. Most Uttarakhand farmers are owner-cultivators. Tenant farming and sharecropping are rare, and landholdings generally small and limited to family farms (Approximately 50% of all landholdings are less than 0.5 hectares in size, and 70% under 1 hectare). As such, the *zamindari* system of big landholders is limited to the plains. Both geography and Pahari cultural heritage has played a role in maintaining traditionally more equitable, if impoverished, land distribution in Uttarakhand.

LIVESTOCK

The hill farming system is characterised by large numbers of livestock. According to the livestock census of 2012, the numbers were as follows:

Livestock	Population
Cattle	2006053
Buffaloes	987775
Goats	1367413
Horses, Mules, Ponnies, Donkeys and Camel	44764

Animals are even reared to produce dung for cultivated land. Animal population tends to increase with human population because every land cultivating household attempts to maintain a pair of bullocks for draught purpose, a cow and a buffalo to produce milk and calves for replacement of bullocks. The landless families also try to rear large number of sheep, goats and buffaloes or cows to get cash income and to augment family food supplies. The productivity level of livestock in the hills is low, the main reason being the degraded condition of the grazing land, the storehouse of livestock fodder. The long dry period (14 months) contributes to the poor milk production. This is attributed to unsuccessful insemination and reluctance of farmers to go for it during milking period. The inadequate availability of nutritious fodder and feeds is the other important factor for low milk production. Livestock subsist mainly on forest floor vegetation. Grazing pressure on an average amounts to 5.67 cattle units per ha which is 2.83 times higher than the carrying capacity of the grazing lands. Overgrazing of forest land is one of the reasons for their degradation.

Bullocks are the only source of power for agriculture in the hills except, of course, human beings. The power developed during ploughing operation by a pair of bullocks is only half of the reported national average.

HORTICULTURE

Uttarakhand produces an estimated 6.63 lakh MT of fruits and 5.85 lakh MT of vegetables. Presently 39 per cent of the cultivable land in the state is under horticulture crops. With market development, as horticultural cultivation becomes more lucrative, it is expected that these rates will remain high and that horticulture will account for larger shares in agricultural output and value.

Currently fruits and vegetables account for 27.2 per cent of the agricultural GVO, less than a percentage point higher than the national average of 26.7 per cent. The situation appears low when compared with the other hill states of Himachal Pradesh and Jammu and Kashmir where fruits and vegetables make up roughly 62 and 58 per cent of the agricultural GVO, respectively.

Agro-processing overall is not well developed and it is estimated that it accounts for a mere 1.5 per cent of total fruits and vegetable production in the state. Recognising the important role that the processing of horticultural products can play in the state, the government of Uttarakhand, as well as the

Centre has provided a number of incentives and support schemes for the growth and development of agro-processing in the state. 19 horticulture-based processing units that came up in the state were subsidised to the tune of Rs. 7214 lakhs. 16 cereals, milk and other commodity-based processing industries received Rs. 9158 lakhs in financial assistance from the state.

Area and Production of Horticultural Crops (Year 2014-15)

S.No.	Items	Unit	Statistics
(A)	**Horticulture Services**		
1.	Infrastructure		
	(i) Horticulture Mobile Teams	No.	289
	(ii) Fruit Preservation Centres	No.	49
	(iii) State Nurseries/Orchards	No.	95
(B)	**Coverage and Production (Provisional)**		
1.	Fruits		
	(i) Area	Hectare	202194
	(ii) Production	M.T.	758238
2.	Vegetables		
	(i) Area	Hectare	65200
	(ii) Production	M.T.	636193
3.	Potato		
	(i) Area	Hectare	25743
	(ii) Production	M.T.	446959
	(iii) Productivity	M.T./Hectare	17.36

FISHING

Fishing is an important part of the economy of Uttarakhand. Apart from agriculture, industries and tourism, fishing also plays on integral role in the economy of the State.

The geography of Uttarakhand presents  topographic variations in many parts of the state, which hinders the prospects of agriculture in Uttarakhand. Agriculture in many parts of Uttarakhand seems to be a nightmare to the inhabitants.

In such an instance, fishing seems to be the most convenient option for the people residing in Uttarakhand. Moreover, many regions of Uttarakhand have ample number of lakes that largely contributes towards the fishing industries.

Among the important fishes found in Uttarakhand are:

- Mulley
- Monstrous Goonch
- Tengra
- Butchwa
- Indian Trout *etc.*

The cities of Nainital, Dehradun, *etc.* are famous for housing a number of lakes. These lakes largely enhance the prospects of fishing in Uttarakhand. Some of the important lakes that has helped in the proliferation of the fishing industry are as follows:

- Bhimtal Lake
- Roopkund
- Naini Lake *etc.*

In fact, the rivers in Uttarakhand also are susceptible towards fishing at Uttarakhand. Some of the rivers that help the fishing industry of Uttarakhand are:

- Ganga
- Bhagirathi
- Alaknanda
- Ramganga *etc.*
- Yamuna
- Sharda
- Kosi

Fish Production in 2014-15

S.No.	Items	Unit	Statistics
1.	Departmental Fish Farms	No.	10
2.	(i) Fish Production	'000 M.T.	4.020
	(ii) Value of Production	₹ Lakh	4686.95
3.	Production of Fish Seed	No Lakh	485.71

10

10 | Energy

THE State has excellent potential for hydropower generation. There are a number of hydro-electric projects on the rivers Yamuna, Bhagirathi, Bhilangana, Alaknanda, Mandakini, Saryu Gauri, Kosi and Kali generating electricity. During 2015-16, the state achieved 100% village electrification.

Nature has given Uttarakhand State unlimited water resources. Natural slope of these rivers has immense potential for generation of power by utilizing the hydro-electric technology. Irrigation Department has built barrages and dams over Ganga, Yamuna and Ram Ganga rivers. By exploring the benefits of hydroelectric projects, Uttarakhand can become a self-reliant State, in power and economy.

POWER

- As on July 2017 the state had an installed power generation capacity of 3313.45 MW.

- The Uttarakhand Power Corporation Limited (UPCL), was established to look after electricity transmission and distribution in the state after Uttarakhand's separation from Uttar Pradesh in 2000.

- The transmission function was later entrusted to Power Transmission Corporation Limited (PTCUL).

- Uttarakhand Jal Vidyut Nigam Limited (UJVNL) controls the state power generation.

- The state's power sector is regulated by the Uttarakhand Electricity Regulatory Commission (UERC).

- Uttarakhand is being developed as an 'energy state' to tap its huge hydro electric power (HEP) potential of over 20,000 MW.

- Uttarakhand has also supported the development of alternate sources of power generation such as solar energy and energy from bio-gas plants. A state-level energy park has also been established in Dehradun.
- Uttarakhand has a small hydro potential of about 1,815.69 MW. Together with large HEP, the projects allocated amount to over 12,700 MW. About 47 locations have already been identified for development by the private sector.

START OF HYDROELECTRIC PROJECTS

For the first time, the construction work of hydroelectric projects in Uttarakhand commenced in 1960. Power was generated in 1965 by constructing Dakpathar barrage, power channel and Dhalipur and Dhakrani powerhouse over Yamuna River.

COMMISSIONED PROJECTS

With the expertise of construction of hydro electric projects by Irrigation Department, following projects have been successfully commissioned in Uttarakhand.

S.No.	Project	Installed capacity (MW)
1	Chhibro	240
2	Khodri	120
3	Dhakrani	33.75
4	Dhalipur	51
5	Kulhal	30
6	Khara	72
7	Maneri Bhali Stage-I	90
8	Chilla	144
9	Pathari	20
10	Kalagarh	198
11	Khatima	41

PROJECTS UNDER CONSTRUCTION

Following projects were initially investigated and framed by Irrigation Department. Infrastructure works were also executed by Irrigation Department and thereafter these projects were transferred to Public Sector Undertaking or Private Sector due to paucity of funds on the part of the Government.

S. No.	Project	Installed Capacity (MW)	Remarks
1.	Tehri Dam Project	2400	Diversion Tunnel and HRT were constructed by Irrigation Department. 1st Phase of Project has been completed by THDC.
2.	Vishnu Prayag Project	400	Infrastructure by Irrigation Department Project Completed by J.P. Associates.
3.	Srinagar Project	330	Infrastructure by Irriagation Department
4.	Maneri Bhali Stage-II	304	Civil works of the project have been completed and generation has started
	Total	3434	

PROJECTS UNDER CONSTRUCTION BUT HELDUP

Following projects are under advance stage of construction by Irrigation Department, but are heldup for the last twelve years or so for want of funds.

S.No.	Project	Installed capacity (MW)	Remarks
1.	Lakhwar Vyasi Project	420	About 40% work is complete
	Total	420	

Main works of Srinagar Project are yet to be started. It is noteworthy to mention that officers from Irrigation Department who opted for public/private sector, have contributed a lot towards these projects.

CHIBRO POWER PLANT (4 × 60MW)

The Power Station is a Run-of-River scheme with an underground power plant. The underground power plant was the first station in the north India and was commissioned in the year 1975. The power station draws water from Ichari dam located on the river Tons, one of the major tributary of river Yamuna.

The water from Ichari dam is fed into the power station through a 6.2 km long Head Race Tunnel (HRT) and the power plant comprising 4 units of 60 MW each with Francis turbines of 84,000 HP output is housed in a rock cavern with the major challenge of maintaining fresh air and safety measures due to constraint in space. The Power Station's Design Energy is 750 MU with a design head of 110 m.

11 Irrigation

$\mathbf{M}$AJOR Part of this State is hilly. Due to this reason, irrigation is not available on the total agricultural land. Irrigation facility is only possible at that place where small channels are constructed. These channels are called 'gool' in Uttarakhand. Putting big obstructions in the way of river the water is turned into the gools. The total length of canals in Uttara-khand is 12,215 km. 5,44,084 hectare arable land is irrigated area. The main canals of Uttarakhand are Upper Ganga canal

> Nature has given Uttarakhand State unlimited water resources. Natural slope of these rivers has immense potential for generation of power by utilizing the hydro-electric technology. Irrigation Department has built barrages and dams over Ganga, Yamuna and Ram Ganga rivers. By exploring the benefits of hydroelectric projects, Uttarakhand can become a self-reliant State, in power and economy.

which emerges at Haridwar and other Sharda canal which emerges at Banbasa. The chief constructive projects for irrigation purposes are as given below :

Tehri Dam Project : This dam is being constructed at Tehri below the confluence of river Bhagirathi and its tributary Bhilangana. According to this project, there is provision to construct 260.5 metre high rock-fill dam from the river-bed. 'Swami-Ramtirtha Sagar' which will be in the backside of the dam,

will have the capacity of 32.2 billion cubic metre water and it will spread 45 km from Bhagirathi valley and 25 km from Bhilangana Valley. The capacity of water in this reservoir will be 2,615 million cubic metre, Consequently 7,400 million cubic metre water of upper Ganga which flows uselessly will be suitably used. From this collected water 2.70 lakh hectare area of Ganga-Yamuna Doab will be irrigated and 340 megawatt hydraulic electricity will be generated at 90% availability. Other dam will be constructed at Koteshwar 22 km below Tehri for continuous flow of water and it will generate 150 megawatt extra hydraulic electricity. According to this project, flood control, development of tourism, fisheries and 500 cusecs potable water will be provided to Delhi. The base of 27 metre deep and 1,100 metre long project has already completed and now Kofer dam is being constructed to save the dam from the danger of flood.

East Ganga Canal Project : According to this project, the main canal having capacity of 4850 cusecs and 48.55 km long has been constructed at the left side of newly constructed Bhim Gonda Top in Haridwar. There is provision to construct five branches–Chandok, Nageena, Nazeebabad, Nahator and Alawalpur from main canal. The lengths of these branches are 155.25 km and the lengths of distribution system are 1488 km. From these branches of canals, the water available in Ganga in rainy season, the facility of irrigation to 105.00 thousand hectare paddy crop of Bijnor and Moradabad districts will be provided.

The expected cost for this project is Rs. 258.48 crore.

Upper Ganga Canal : This canal has been constructed from the right bank of Ganga river near Haridwar. Its construction began in 1842 and finished in 1856. The main branches of it are-Maat branch, Deoband and Anoopshahar branch. For additional facility of irrigation for Kharif crop, modernisation of above-mentioned branches is proposed. The expected cost of this project is Rs. 13.26 crore.

Jamrani Dam Project : Terai and Bhabhar region of Nainital is one of the fertile lands. Due to the lack of irrigation facilities, the agriculture has not developed properly. Therefore, seeing the problems of food and potable water and bring irrigation facilities, Jamrani Dam Project in Nainital district under its first phase Gola Barrage on Gola river near Kathgodam, construction of helper canal, redemption of present canal system, *etc.* and in its second phase, the construction of Roller compacted concrete Barrage are proposed. By the construction of this dam, the irrigation facility for 60,600 hectare land will be available and 15 megawatt hydro-electricity will be generated. By the construction of this project, potable water in Bhabhar area of Haldwani, Kathgodam and Nainital will be made available.

The work of first phase is complete. The construction of main dam could not be started.

Sharda Subsidiary Project : The main works which will be taken according to this project are–1,003 metre long dam on Ghaghra, 28 km long connecting canal, 811 metre long dam on Sharda river, 269 km long feeder canal, construction of 6,450 km long distribution system and construction of 2,570 km long canal.

Above-mentioned works are to be completed in five phases. First and second phases are complete. The works on remaining three phases are going on.

12 | Migration

A major trend in the livelihood pattern of people of Uttarakhand is the tremendous amount of permanent migration taking place from all the hill Blocks. Seasonal migration was reported to be an integral part of the life of the people of Uttarakhand since ancient times. However, after the 1962 Indo-China War, migration of the Shaukas into Tibet has stopped. A decreasing livestock population has also drastically reduced migration for transhumance. Permanent migration is reported to be negligible. Thus, the major type of migration is of a semi-permanent nature which started only after 1920.

In recent decades, semi-permanent migration in Uttarakhand has increased after the 1962 Indo-China War after which the number of recruitment centres into the army in Uttarakhand were increased. The better accessibility and communication following the war and an increasing tilt towards commercialisation of the economy in Uttarakhand increased  to a large extent the migration for employment into the army. This situation has reached such a state today that it is estimated that out of a total population of Kumaon, 1.27 lakhs persons are employed in the military and paramilitary forces. On an average 1400 people every year join the army, thus 1 out of every 19 households in Kumaon has a person employed in the army. In Pithoragarh this incidence is even higher with 1 out of every 2 households having a person employed in the army and 1 out of every three household having a pensioner. The profile of Garhwal is similar. A study by S.S. Khanka found that the main reason for migration was insufficient income in 92% of the samples studied. Unemployment (6%) and unstable occupation (1%) were other reasons. It was found that migration occurred mainly due to push factors rather than pull factors. The majority of the migrants are reported to be between 15-35 years of age and largely with formal education. 85% of the sample studied sent money-orders back home, most of which is used for current use. In a large majority of cases the increases in the household income due to migration was found to be more than 5 times. The study reports that the average labour required per hectare of land cultivated was 1.77 person units. Thus, if household labour was in excess to this, the increase in productivity is only marginal.

Seasonal migration in Almora was 78% and 98% in Byans area in 1901 (mainly by Shaukas of Byans). However, after a closure of Tibet trade and consequent settling down of the Shaukas, this seasonal migration has almost stopped. The author has worked out that the out migration from Uttarakhand based on 1981 figures is 29.7%.

13 Growth in Uttarakhand : The Past and the Future

FOLLOWING its inception as an independent state in 2000-01, the Uttarakhand economy has been growing at very high rates in the last few years. This has led to expectations of continued high growth rate during the Twelfth Plan period as well. However, any objective projection of future growth rates has to be based on a careful analysis of the long-run trends in the economy. The relevant period for this exercise is the era following the reforms initiated in the Indian economy. Specifically, the date for the period 1993-94, up to the present needs to be analysed in order to generate projections for the Twelfth Plan period.

Trends in sectoral and sub-sectoral growth in the Uttarakhand economy since 1993-04, show two distinctly different kinds of growth dynamics. There are six sub-sectors that exhibit steady and unchanging growth dynamics for the whole period. These are *(i)* Agriculture, *(ii)* Forestry, *(iii)* Fishery, *(iv)* Mining, *(v)* Real Estate, Ownership of Dwellings and Business Services, and *(vi)* Banking and

Insurance. On the other hand, the remaining seven sub-sectors show a distinct jump in growth rates since the time the state was established, *i.e.*, 2000-01. These are: *(i)* Manufacturing *(ii)* Construction *(iii)* Electricity, Gas and Water *(iv)* Trade, Hotels and Restaurants *(v)* Transport, Storage and Communications *(vi)* Other Services and *(vii)* Public Administration. These high rates of growth are partly due to the small base of these sectors while other factors like better administration and governance, together with fiscal incentives for private participation in these sectors, are also important. While some of these factors will remain significant even in the long run, others will have a more temporary impact on the growth rates. Clearly the capacity to sustain high growth rates will depend on whether the long-run factors remain more relevant than the temporary factors in the future.

In order to generate growth projections that capture this changing economic behaviour exhibited by the state following its inception, it is useful to define alternative growth scenarios. In fact, the most feasible outcomes for Uttarakhand for the Twelfth Plan period can be taken care of by three alternative scenarios. These may be termed as the Optimistic Scenario, the Pessimistic Scenario and the Realistic Scenario. These scenarios are defined for the sub-sectoral growth behaviour and then aggregated to generate the sectoral (agriculture, industry and services) and aggregate GSDP growth behaviour for Uttarakhand.

14 | Tourism

THE tourism industry is a major contributor to the economy of Uttarakhand, with the Corbett National Park and Tiger Reserve and the nearby hill-stations of Nainital, Mussourie, Almora and Ranikhet being among the most frequented destinations of India. To this region, long called "abode of the gods" *(Devbhoomi)*, also belong some of the holiest Hindu shrines, and for more than a thousand years, pilgrims have been visiting the 4-dham temples at Gangotri, Yamunotri, Badrinath, Kedarnath. In the hope of salvation and purification from sin people also visit Haridwar and Rishikesh where are some of the major spiritual and yoga centres of India. Gangotri (the source of Ganga) and Yamunotri (source of Yamuna) are revered by many. Besides these most popular pilgrim centres, the state has an abundance of temples and shrines, references to most of which can be found in Hindu scriptures and legends. The architecture of most of these temples is typical of the region and slightly different from other parts of India, the ancient temples at Jogeshwar being the most prominent for their distinct architectural features.

With great views of the Himalaya, apart from the well known pilgrimages and hill stations, it offers wonderful travel destinations to lesser known places and offers much in adventure activities, like skiing, yachting, trekking and mountaineering. There are excellent ski slopes at Auli, Dayara Bugyal, Mundali and Munsiari. Watersports such as rafting can be tried out on the Yamuna Alaknanda, Bhagirathi, Bhilangana, Mandakini and the Mahakali. There is a sailing club at Nainital. The state offers excellent trekking terrain and some of the famous treks take you to the Valley of Flowers and Pindari, Sunderdhunga and Kafni glaciers.

The Government of India has awarded the National Tourism Award in the category of Special Award for Efforts in the Development and Promotion of Tourism to the State Government of Uttarakhand, in 2000.

Focused, planned and time bound development of trek routes, yatra routes and adventure sports such as river rafting, paragliding, skiing, mountaineering are planned by the state.

Haridwar

The Himalayan region of Uttarakhand is a popular tourism destination which possesses Alpine conditions represented by cold winters with prolonged snowfall, considerable rainfall in the monsoon and pleasant summers.

Rishikesh

This climate is the most significant factor in providing the state with its only livelihood, that is tourism.

The scope of tourism is considerable in this state, whether it is nature, wildlife, adventure or pilgrimage. The most popular destinations in Uttarakhand are:

- Haridwar
- Rishikesh
- Dehradun
- Mussourie
- Almora
- Kedarnath
- Badrinath
- Yamunotri
- Gangotri
- Nainital
- Ranikhet
- Pithoragarh

Kedarnath

If a tourist is adventurous and prefers to face a new thrills, he can opt for high-and-low-altitude trekking, river rafting, para gliding, hang-gliding, mountaineering, skiing and similar other alternatives.

Gangotri Gomukh Waterfall

Tourism reaches its peak season at the time of fairs and festivals of the Garhwal and Kumaon region like:

- Hatkalika Fair
- Tapkeshwar Fair

Nainital Lake

- Surkhanda Devi Mela
- Kunjapuri Fair
- Lakhawar Village Fair
- Mata Murti Ka Mela
- Uttarayani Mela
- Shravan Mela (Jageshwar)
- Kartik Poornima
- Kasar Devi fair
- Nanda Devi Mela

Matamurti Fair

TOURISM IN UTTARAKHAND IS PROMOTED BY GOOD TRANSPORT NETWORK:

Jolly Grant close to Dehradun is the single airport. There are frequent flights to Delhi.

Dehradun, Haridwar and Kathgodam are principal railway stations linked to most areas by regular trains. However, for those visiting places at considerable heights, trekking and road routes are the only option.

Significant locales are connected by roads although places high up are often inaccessible due to landslides and snowfall. National Highways 58, 73, 74 and 87 link important places in the country.

Frequent bus services link Delhi and other major areas of North India with Dehradun.

Tourism is the principal source of revenue in the state of Uttarakhand.

MINISTRY OF TOURISM

Ministry of tourism of Uttarakhand is responsible for maintaining and generating revenue from tourism in the state. It is also the responsibility of tourism ministry of Uttarakhand to formulate plans for increasing revenue from tourism industry. The ministry has to decide the rules and regulations for the efficient working of the tourism industry.

Tourism ministry of Uttarakhand has created two tourism corporations for Garhwal and Kumaon region named as Garhwal Mandal Vikas Nigam Limited and Kumaon Mandal Vikas Nigam Limited so as to offer quality service to the tourists.

Moreover, these two regions consists of most of the star tourist attractions. Through these corporations, the ministry of tourism of Uttarakhand is trying to woo more tourists in these regions by offering various tourist packages. These tourist packages range from pilgrimage, adventure sports to wildlife tours, *etc.* Tourists can book this on line. This is how it is adding up revenue to the state economy.

The ministry of tourism in Uttarakhand runs its own fleet of transport and offers accommodation in its own tourist rest houses. These generate more revenue to the state while to the tourists it gives satisfaction of being secure under the government roof.

The functioning of Uttarakhand ministry of tourism is commendable for generating the highest revenue through tourism. Moreover, the ministry has indirectly helped the other industries of Uttarakhand such as small scale industries and Gramodhyogs. Tourists come and shop products of these industries thereby generating more revenue to the state. Due to increase in tourism, the hotel industry in Uttarakhand is on the rise. Hence, the hard work of the Tourism Ministry of Uttarakhand is paying off in the form of revenue that is earned by the state.

MAJOR TOURIST ATTRACTIONS

I. Nature Tourism:

(a) Wildlife: Askot Sanctuary, Corbett National Park, Govind Wildlife Sanctury, Nanda Devi National Park, Rajaji National Park, Valley of Flowers, Assan Barrage.

(b) Glaciers: Bandarpunch Glacier, Chorbari Bamak Glacier, Dokriani Glacier, Doonagiri Glacier, Gangotri Glacier, Pindari Glacier, Maiktoli Glacier, Sunderdhunga Glacier, Milam Glacier, Ralam Glacier, Namik Glaciers, Khatling Glaciers, Nandadevi Glacier, Satopnath, Bhagirathi-Khark Glacier, Tiprabamak Glacier.

Rajaji National Park

II. Pilgrimage Tourism:

(a) Yatras: Char Dham Yatra, Nanda Devi Yatra, Kailash Mansarovar Yatra

(b) Pilgrimage Centres:

(i) Almora: Doonagiri Temple, Jageshwar Temple, Chital Temple, Hairakhan.

Kailash Mansarovar Yatra

(ii) Bageshwar: Bagnath Temple, Chandika Temple, Shri Haru Temple, Gauri Udiyar.

(iii) Chamoli: Badrinath, Hemkund Saheb, Gopeshwar, Prayags.

(iv) Champawat: Baleshwar Temple, Gwal Devta, Devidhura, Kranteshwar Mahadev, Meetha Reetha Saheb, Purnagiri.

Hemkund Saheb (Chamoli)

(v) Dehradun: Bhadraj Temple, Surkhanda Devi, Jwalaji Temple, Nag Devta Temple, Parkasheshwar Temple, Bharat Mandir, Kailash Niketan Mandir, Satya Narayan Temple, Shatrughan Temple, Neelkanth Mahadev.

Nag Devta Temple

(vi) Haridwar: Har ki Pauri, Sapt Rishi Ashram and Sapt Sarovar, Mansa Devi Temple, Chandi Devi Temple, Maya Devi Temple, Daksha Mahadev Temple.

(vii) Nainital: Garjiya Devi Temple, Naina Devi Temple, Seeta Bani Temple.

Mansa Devi Temple

(viii) Pauri: Siddhibali Temple, Durga Devi Temple, Medanpuri Devi Temple, Shri Koteshwar Mahadev, Tarkeshwar Mahadev, Keshorai Math, Kamleshwar Temple, Shankar Math, Devalgarh, Dhar Devi.

(ix) Pithoragarh: Dhwaj Temple, Narayan Ashram, Patal Bhubaneshwar, Thal Kedar, Kapileshwar Mahadev.

Naina Devi Temple

(x) Rudraprayag: Kedarnath Temple, Shankaracharya Samadhi, Gaurikund, Son Prayag, Panch Kedar, Madmaheshwar, Tungnath, Koteshwar, Guptkashi.

(xi) Tehri Garhwal: Surkhanda Devi Temple.

(xii) Udham Singh Nagar: Atariya Temple, Nanak Matta, Purnagiri, Chaiti.

Om Parvat (Pithoragarh)

(xiii) **Uttarkashi:** Gangotri, Yamunotri.

III. Adventure Tourism:

(a) Skiing: Auli, Mundali, Dayara Bagyal, Munsya.

(b) Water Sports:

(i) Still water sports: Assan Barrage Water Sports Resort, Nainital Lake Paradise, Nanaksagar Matta.

(ii) Rafting:

(a) Garhwal: River Yamuna: Barkot to Bernigad, Damta to Yamuna Bridge, Mori to Tuni (Khoonigad). River Alaknanda: Kaliasaur to Srinagar, Srinagar to Bagwan, Kaliasaur to Rishikesh. River Bhagirathi: Matli to Dunda, Harsil to Uttarkashi, Dharasu to Chham, Jangla to Jhala, Bhaldyana to Tehri. River Bhilangana: Ghansali to Gadolia. River Mandakini: Chandrapuri to Rudraprayag.

(b) Kumaon: River Maha Kali, Kaudiyala Rafters Camp.

Uttarkashi

River Bhagirathi

River Alaknanda

15 | Char Dham Yatra

TRADITIONALLY, the journey (yatra) is done from the west to the east-starting from Yamunotri, then proceeding to Gangotri and finally to Kedarnath and Badrinath.

Yamunotri and Gangotri fall under Uttarkashi district in Garhwal region of Uttarakhand. Badrinath falls under Chamoli and also house three out of five Panch Kedar, Panch Badris, Sacred Sikh shrine of Hemkund Sahib Skiing paradise Auli and the legendary Valley of Flowers. The holy pilgrimage of Kedarnath nestles in Rudraprayag.

Although Char Dham are accessible through a network of motorable roads, arduous trails remain the ancient sanctuaries of faith for a fulfilling experience. The usual starting point is Rishikesh/Haridwar.

> त्रैलोक्य दुःख दलनाय समागतो यो
> नारायणो नरसखा बदरीबनान्ते।।
> सिद्धैः समृद्ध चरितैः समपास्यमानो
> सोऽय तनोतु तव मंगल कीर्तिलाभम्।।
>
> कण्ठे यस्य विराजते हि गरलम् गंगाजलं मस्तके,
> बमागे, गिरिराज राज तनयां जाया भवानी स्थिता।
> नन्दीस्कन्द गर्णधिनाथ सहिताः केदारनाथः प्रभुः
> केदाराचल सस्थितों हि सतंतू कुर्वन्तुनो मंगलम्।

Yamunotri (The Sacred Jewel of the Himalayas) The shrine of Yamunotri, source of the river Yamuna, is the westernmost shrine in the Garhwal Himalayas, perched atop a flank of Bandar

Yamunotri Dham

Gangotri Dham

Kedarnath Dham

Badrinath Dham

Poonch peak (3615 m) and situated opposite to Gangotri. The actual source, a frozen lake of ice and glacier (Champasar glacier) located on the Kalind mountain at the height of 4421 m above sea level, about 1 km further up, is not frequented generally as it is not accessible and hence the shrine has been located on the foot of the hill. The tiny Yamuna has icy cold water and its absolute innocence and the infantile purity heightens that deep feeling of reverence, Yamunotri for the devout.

The temple of Yamuna is on the left bank of Yamuna constructed by Maharaja Pratap Shah of Tehri Garhwal. The deity is made of black marble. The Yamuna like Ganga has been elevated to the status of divine mother for the Hindus and has been held responsible for nurturing and developing the Indian civilization.

According to the legend ancient sage Asit muni had his hermitage here. All his life, he bathed daily both in Ganga and Yamuna. Unable to go to Gangotri during his old age, a stream of Ganga appeared opposite Yamunotri for him.

Close to the temple are hot water springs gushing out from the mountain cavities. Suryakund is the the most important kund. Near the Surya Kund there is a shila called Dibya-Shila, which is worshipped before puja is offered to the deity. Devotees prepare rice and potatoes to offer at the shrine by dipping them in these hot water springs, tied in muslin cloth. Rice so cooked is taken back home as prasadam.

> The daughter of the Sun god, Surya and consciousness, Sangya the birthplace of the Yamuna is the Champasar Glacier (4421m). Just below the Bandarpunch mountain. The mountain adjacent to the river's source is dedicated to her father, and is called Kalinda Parvat. Kalinda being another name for Surya. Yamuna is known for her frivolousness, a trait that she developed because as per a common story - Yamuna's mother could never make eye contact with her dazzling husband.

The pandas (pujaris) of Yamunotri come from the village of Kharsali near Jankichatti. They are the administrators of the sacred place and perform religious rites well–versed in the Shastras.

The temple and the place opens every year on the auspicious day of the akshya-tritya, which generally falls during the last week of April, or the early first week of May. The temple always closes on the sacred day of Diwali mid-Oct.-1st week of November, with a brief ceremony, the temple staff return to their villages and for the rest of the time the valley is gripped in no man silence and covered with white sheet of show. With melting of snow next summer, temple re-opens to blissful happiness of thousands of visitors again.

The trek to Yamunotri is truly spectacular dominated by a panorama of rugged peaks and dense forests.

LAKHAMANDAL

Lakhamandal

Located on the banks of river Yamuna, Lakhamandal is known both for its historical and mythological significance as well as cultural & architectural richness. Some remains of the temples dedicated to Shiva, Parshuram and five Pandavas made of shiny granite-like material still attract. Some statues are also now in the custody of the archaeological department in a temporary museum. Historians identify the place with the epic Laxagriha (house of wax) made by Duryodhan (Kaurava) in a conspiracy to kill Pandavs.

GMVN organises Kalsi Lakhamandal Trek for 7 days around the year offering architectural richness of the Jaunsar-Bhabar region and cultural insight into Jaunsaris tribe.

SURYAKUND

There are a number of thermal springs in the vicinity of the temple, which flow into numerous pools. The most important of these Suraj Kund is known for its very high temperature of 190° F. Pilgrims cook rice and potatoes here to offer to deity in the temple. Near Surya Kund there is a slab of stone known as Dibya Shila or the slab of divine light. This slab is worshipped before puja is offered to Yamuna.

JANKICHATTI

216 km from Rishikesh, this is the last balting point en route Yamunotri. This is the place where all pilgrims have to return for the night halt, the same day because of the extremely limited accommodation options available at Yamunotri. The 6 km trek to Yamunotri from here is a steep climb and thus has to be started on early morning to return to Jankichatti for night halt, the same day.

Ponies and dandies can be arranged a day before for negotiating the trek for those unable to cope with trek physically.

The thermal springs here offer a spectacular sight and a refreshing bath for the pilgrims. Surrounding the places are lush valley with a profusion of conifers, rhododenrons, cacti and several species of Himalayan shrubs and one can enjoy panoramic view of the fabled snow-clad Yamunotri peaks.

During the Yatra season temporary shops are set up selling things of daily needs. Services of a post office and police station is available during the season. Stalls selling pure and simple Indian vegetarian food are always available.

HANUMANCHATTI

In olden times all halting places en route were called Chattis and some of these still retain their traditional names like Hanumanchatti. Hanuman-chatti is the last motorhead on way to Yamunotri and is the hub of activities in season. It is a place

Hanumanchatti

of confluence of Hanuman Ganga and Yamuna rivers, from where the trek to Dodi Tal (3,307 m) starts. The trek from Hanumanchatti starts with a gentle climb and the 7 km trek through Phoolchatti Jankichatti is most enjoyable as the path trails its way through wooded hills and meadows shaded with beautiful green, while the fragrance of the Himalayan trees and shrubs permeate the cool mountain *etc.*

SAYANACHATTI

It is from Barkot that the road to Yamunotri starts wending its way along the banks of the Yamuna, and the road from Mussoorie and Kalsi meets here. The road from Barkot leads on along the banks of the Yamuna through a valley of lush vegetation and the pretty hamlets of Gangani and Kuthnaur, to a place called Sayanachatti, some 29 km away. It is a small village, nestling in the woods along the bank of river making a lovely sight.

CHAMBA

A sylvan spot on way to Tehri that offers an excellent view of the Himalayan peaks. Situated at an altitude of 1676 m. On a clear day one can see the impressive Bandarpoonch Peak and the snow on the mountain ranges. The way is colourful as 21 m from Chamba one comes to the famous temple of

Surkanda Devi, perched atop a hill, and then continues on through a fruit belt where Apples, Apricots and other Himalayan fruits are grown, to Mussoorie, Chamba is an ideal summer retreat.

Chamba

17 km from Chamba and 79 kms from Rishikesh is Dobata which in the local dialect means a function. It is here that travellers to Yamunotri & Gangotri abandon the road to Tehri and take the one to Dharasu (41 km from Dobata). Round the year, a 4 day trek, Devi Darshan Trek organised by GMVN entails seeing 3 sidha peeths – Chamba, Surkanda Devi and Kunjapuri-Durga Goddess. Rishikesh-Chandrabadni-Chandra-Surkanda Devi – Dhanolti – Kunjapuri.

BARKOT

40 km from Brahmakhal at an altitude of 1280 m, Barkot is the area rich in the forests of pines, cypresses, and rhododendrons. The eternal snows of Bandarpoonch peak offer a spectacular view. During the period from June to mid September the adjoining hills have trees laden with fruits such as apples, apricots, pears and walnuts. Barkot is the last populated town on the Yamunotri route and also a marketplace.

NARENDRA NAGAR

16 km from Rishikesh, it was once the capital of the old state of Tehri and houses the palace of the former Maharaja, Narendra Shah of Tehri. Narendra Nagar is a pictureseque hill resort situated through such dense forest slopes on way to Yamunotri Gangotri.

GANGOTRI (The Eternal Gift of Bhagirathi Penance)

Gangotri (with Bhagirathi)

The picturesque pilgrimage in the hinterlands of the Himalayas is the most sacred spot where Ganga, the stream of life, touched earth for the first time. According to mythology, Goddess Ganga, the daughter of heaven, manifested herself in the form a river to absolve the sins of king Bhagirath's predecessors, following his severe penance of 5500 years, Lord Shiva received into his matted locks to minimize the impact of her fall. The river itself begins at Gangotri which literally means Ganga Uttari or Ganga descending. She came to be called Bhagirathi at her legendary source. The Shrine of Gangotri situated at an elevation of 3200 m above sea level amidst captivating surroundings along the right bank of Bhagirathi is 100 km from Uttarkashi.

The temple was constructed in the early 18th century by a Gorkha Commander Amar Singh Thapa. The existing temple is said to be the one reconstructed by the Jaipur dynasty. Every year thousands of pilgrims throng the sacred shrine between May and October. The Pujaris and brahmins are from the village of Mukhwa. The water from Gangotri is carried to offer to Lord Shiva. It is believed that this water has amrit (nectar) in it and will soothe the throat of Shiva who gulp the poison.

According to mythology King Sagar after slaying the demons on earth staged an Aswamedh Yagna to proclaim his supremacy. The King's 60,000 sons born of Queen Sumati and one son Asamanjas of Queen Kesani were to accompany the horse. Lord Indra fearing loss of his supremacy stole the horse and tied it to the ashram of ancient sage Kapil who was then deep into meditation.

Ganga River

On their search for horse, the 60,000 sons stormed the ashram of Kapil and just before the attack on him the sage opened his eyes and reduced all the 60,000 sons of King Sagar except Asamanjas to ashes. King Sagar's grandson Anshuman was successful in recovering the horse from Kapil and was told that those 60,000 burnt will attain heavenly abode if Ganga is brought down from heaven and their ashes were cleaned by its water. Then the great task of bringing Ganga to earth started. Anshuman failed and so did his son Dilip but his grandson Bhagirath succeeded.

The intense meditation made Ganga to descend from heaven and in order that the earth is not flooded, it remained suspended in the Coils of Lord Shiva's hair. Shiva pleased with King Bhagirath, released Ganga in seven streams – the most sacred stream on earth came to be known as Bhagirathi. King Sagar's 60,000 sons' ashes were touched with Ganga water and thus they were bestowed with eternal rest in heaven.

The waters of dozens of rivers, rivulets and lakes enhance the rich heritage of this Himalayan state. Among the numerous rivers & streams, the Ganga, Yamuna, Alaknanda and Kali are of great religious significance. In India, the rivers are veritable gifts from Mother India itself. Like her they, too, are all women, and again like her they too, beat a touch of divinity. Rivers have always been an inseparable part of Hinduism.

Ganga to a Hindu is not only the 'River of Life' but also, at the same time, 'The River of Death' for he longs to die beside it, or at the very least to have his ashes after cremation cast in its water. It is believed that the holy waters of this river washes away the sins and cleanses the soul of lesser mortals. Some of the facts about the quality of Ganga's water cannot be lightly discussed. Scientists have or say they have established how the water will keep for a year in bottles and that cholera germs die in it within a few hours, or even that a tank reputed to be fed from the Ganga has the power of dissolving human bones within three days. Geologists firmly believe that the mineral contents of the water also makes the difference. A Sanskrit verse that a Hindu recites at the time of taking the dip is as under.

गंगेच यमुनेचैव गोदावरी सरस्वती
नमदे सिंधु कावेरी जले अस्मिन सनिधमू कुरू

O Ganga, O Yamuna, and also Godavari & Saraswati
and Narmada Sindhu and Kaveri, by your waters
I purify myself. This hymn to the rivers is also a hymn to the nation.

GANGOTRI TEMPLE

As the legend goes, King Bhagirath used to worship Lord Shiva at the sacred stone, near which this 18th century temple is located. The slab on which King Bhagirath is believed to have meditated is called Bhagirathi Shila.

The Mother Ganga is worshipped as Goddess and the holy river in the temple. Before performing the puja rituals, a holy dip in the Ganga flowing nearby the temple is a must. The pujaris belong to Brahmin community from Mukhwa village. Ten of them are selected by rotation every year to perform all the functions covering the temple and they also perform the duties of pandas.

Gangotri Temple

The shrine of Gangotri, like Yamunotri, opens during the last week of April or the first week of May, on the auspicious day of Akshaya – Tritiya. The temples opening is preceded by a special puja of Ganga both inside the temple as well as on the river bank. The temple's closes on the day of Diwali followed by a formal closing ceremony amidst a row of oil lamps. By this time, Gangotri is covered with snow. It is believed that the Goddess retreats to Mukhawa, her winter abode (12 km downstream). The temple staff return to leave behind Gangotri to the care of Mother Ganga only to reach Gangotri next summer to set the temple bells chiming again and perform the usual puja rituals.

SUBMERGED SHIVLING

The natural rock shivling submerged in the river, is an amazing sight reinforcing the power of the divine. According to mythology, Lord Shiva sat at this spot to receive the Ganga in his matted locks. The Shivling is visible in the early winters when the water level goes down.

GAUMUKH

The Gangotri Glacier, which is situated at a height of 4255 m above sea level, is nearly 24 km in length and 6-8 km in width. It starts from beyond the Chaukhamba cluster of snow peaks, in the neighbourhood of Badrinath and extends as far as Gaumukh. Almost 16 km northeast of Gangotri, Gaumukh is generally accepted as the physical source of holy river. It is held in high esteem by the devouts who do not miss the opportunity to have holy dip in the bone chilling ice water. Locals are of the opinion that the glacier is receding at the rate of 5 m a year. Several pilgrims trek up to the source to offer prayers either on foot or on ponies. The verdant valleys, dense forests and towering peaks offer excellent trekking and mountaineering opportunities.

Gaumukh

The trek of Gaumukh is enough to hypnotise one with mesmerising view of Bhagirathi peaks, the ranges of Shivling. Chirbasa, 9 km from Gangotri, is a beautiful site with its blue pine. This popular camping site offers glimpses of glaciated heights of Gaumukh. 14 km trek from Gangotri, Bhojwasa is the place with its forest of Bhojpatra trees. The paper like bark of this tree locally known as Bhojpatra was used as a substitute for paper for writing in ancient times.

DAYARA BUGYAL

Dayara is an another paradise for nature lovers in the Uttarkashi district and approachable from Bhatwari. The road to Dayara Bugyal branches of near Bhatwari on Uttarkashi Gangotri road about 28 km from Uttarkashi. Situated at an elevation of about 3048 m, this vast meadow is second to none in natural beauty. During winter it provides excellent ski slopes over an area of 28 sq.km. The view of the Himalayas from here is breathtaking. From here one can also trek down to Dodital which is about 22 km away through dense forest. Another attraction en route is the famous Sheshnag temple.

GMVN organises a 10-day summer Uttarkashi Panwali Kantha Kedarnath trek through seven Bugyal of Panwali Kantha on the ancient pilgrim trail from Gangotri to Kedarnath. Rishikesh-Uttarkashi-Belak-Budhakedar-Bhairon Ghati-Ghuttu-Panwali Kantha-Triyuginarayan-Gaurikund-Kedarnath-Rishikesh.

NANDANVAN TAPOVAN

These two spots are situated opposite the Gangotri glacier, further up from Gaumukh. Nandanvan is the base camp of Bhagirathi peaks from where the visitor can have a superb view of the majestic Shivling peak. A trek across the south of the Gangotri Glacier leads to Tapovan, known for its beautiful meadows that encircle the base of the Shivling peak. GMVN organises an 8 day summer Gangotri Nandanvan Tapovan trek. Rishikesh-Gangotri-Bhojwasa-Tapovan-Nandanvan-Bhojwasa-Gangotri-Rishikesh.

KEDARTAL

18 km from Gangotri, negotiable through a rough & tough mountain trail is the spectacular and enchanting lake of Kedartal. The lake is crystal clear with the mightyThalayasagar, Sphatikling peak forming a splendid backdrop. The place is about 100 m high and is the base camp for trekking to Thalayasagar, Jogin, Bhrigupanth and other peaks. The trek to Kedartal is testing and

Kedartal

one needs to have local guide and make all arrangements in advance.

HAR-KI-DOON

The hanging valley of Gods - Har-Ki-Doon is trekkers, paradise in the least explored areas of Garhwal. This valley is a treat for botanist, bird watcher and explorer. At the backdrop is glistening snow clad Swargarohi peak and it has forests of pine, deodar and other conifers bordering vast stretches of meadows. Har-ki-Doon falls within the Govind Pashu Vihar. Duryodhana, the Kaurava

Prince is traditionally worshipped as main deity in the Fateh Parvat region. This region is separated from Himachal Pradesh by river Tons. Jaundhar Glacier (4300 m) is also of great interest just about five kilometres from Har-ki-Doon. GMVN organises a nine-day trek in this area.

UTTARKASHI

Created in 1960, at an elevation of 1158 m on the bank of river Bhagirathi, this picturesque town is also the district headquarter. It is located in a wide stretch of a valley. Uttarkashi is an important pilgrimage centre, equated with Varanasi or Kashi in divinity. The town is situated between Varuna and Assi streams with ghats bearing the same names as those of Kashi.

Uttarkashi

Topographically, the district is mountainous but a network of roads has made all parts easily accessible. Rishikesh is at a distance of 145 km.

From the religious point of view, the place is important because the temple of Lord Vishwanath is located here along with other important temples like Ekadash Rudra, Bhairon, Gyaneshwar, and Goddess Kuteti Devi. Shiva is the presiding deity at this ancient temple of Lord Vishwanath. Description about this temple is given in Kedarkhand (Skandpuran). A massive old brass trident (26ft high) is erected here supposedly by son Guh of King Gyaneshwar.

5 km away is the famous Nehru Institute of Mountaineering. The first Indian Woman to scale Mount Everest, Bachendri Pal, hailing from a small village Nakuri, received her basic training in mountaineering from this very institute.

Close by at Ujeliare are a number of ashrams and temples. The town houses a historical building constructed by Peshwa ruler Nana Sahib Dhundu during the exile. Every year on the occasion of Magh Mela (14th Jan.) people visit Uttarkashi to take a holy dip in Bhagirathi along with the idol of their local deities.

The fair lasts for seven days with colourfully dressed women bedecked with traditional ornaments and men and chilidren throng the town from the surrounding villages. They sing and dance merrily to the accompanying musical instruments enhancing the festive spirits.

MANERI

13 km form Uttarkashi on way to Gangotri. Maneri is the site of a dam across the Bhagirathi river, from where water is fed to the turbines through an 8 km

long tunnel at Tiloth in Uttarkashi. The resonant lake at Maneri has added to the charm of the place.

HARSIL

Harsil

73 km from Uttarkashi on way to Gangotri, this sylvan hamlet is famous for its natural beauty. Situated amidst the incredible beauty of mountain peaks, 2620 m high. Harsil is the quiet resort to discover the undiscovered stretches of green, grassy land and enjoy the surroundings.

SATTAL

It means seven lakes, is situated just above Dharali, 2 km beyond Harsil. The 7 km trek is rewarding, as this group of lakes is situated amids beautiful natural surrounding. It also provides a lovely camping site.

GANGNANI

Gangnani

43 km from Uttarkashi and 14 km from Bhatwari, Gangnani is noted for its thermal springs where one can take a bath for relaxation and rejuvenation. It is a small paradise with its spectacular views and tranquil surroundings offer peace and solitude.

The place can best be taken up as a place for meditation. Further 18 km ascent, is Sukhi Top at an altitude of 2744 m offering splendid view of the snowcapped Himalayas and trailing waterfalls on the opposite mountains. It is also known for its seasonal fruit harvest of apples, apricots, *etc.*

LANKA

11 km from Harsil at an altitude of 2758 m the route to the Lanka is along a road shaded by deodars and across the turbulent Bhagirathi. Lanka till 1985 was the last motorhead on the route to Gangotri, until a bridge on Jahnvi, a tributary of Bhagirathi, came up – perhaps the highest in the world. The road from Lanka to Gangotri is a gradual ascent through dense forest of giant deodar trees

DODITAL

123 km, the origin of this Tal is from the natural springs and the source of river Asi Ganga. The road from Uttarkashi to Gangotri, bifurcates after 4 km at Gangotri from Uttarkashi and vehicles can go up to Kalyani, 7 km, further up from where Agoda is 5 km away at an altitude of 2286 m. The trek from these ascends gradually through thick forests and beautiful mountainous scenery. Dodi Tal is 16 km further from Agoda, situated at an elevation of 3307 m. The lakes is sparkling and crystal clear, surrounded by forests. The famous and rare Himalayan trout are found in abundance in the lake.

Dodital

Permits for fishing can be obtained from the Divisional Forest Officer, Uttarkashi. From here one can trek to Hanumanchatti and then to Yamunotri. By the side of Dodital there is a Forest Rest House and a Log Cabin. GMVN organises Dodital Yamunotri Trek, a 9-day summer season venture. Rishikesh-Uttarkashi-Agora-Dodital-Seema-Hanumanchatti-Yamunotri-Barkot Rishikesh.

NACHIKETA TAL

Nachiketa, the devout son of sage Uddalak, is said to have created this lake, hence the name 29 km from Uttarkashi is Chaurangikhal and from here a 3 km trek through lush green forests takes one to the tranquil spot of Nachiketa Tal. There is greenery all around and a small temple at the bank of the lake gives it a serene look. PWD Inspection House at Chaurangikhal is available.

BHAIRONGHATI

Bhaironghati

On the way to Gangotri Bhaironghati is the place to stay and enjoy the mountainous landscape. A temple of Bhairon Devta here is visited by scores of pilgrims. The temple of Bhairon Devta is gateway God of Gangotri. 9 km away from here is the last base camp for Gangotri. The awe-inspiring lofty peaks, deep gorge of Jahanvi & Bhagirathi rivers with bridges at the considerable altitude from river level flowing below and the towering deodar trees provide a rare natural bonanza. GMVN-TRH, Forest, Rest House and PWD Inspection House provide accommodation facility here.

KEDARNATH (The Celestial Jyotirlingam)

At Yumnotri & Gangotri, the pilgrims are cleansed body and soul and with having achieved purity in that sense, pilgrimage to Sri Kedarnath becomes most rewarding. It is also customary to worship Lord Shiva with water of Ganga, which pilgrims going from Gangotri as well take some there to Kedarnath.

Kedarnath Jyotirlingam

Kedarnath is the seat of Lord Shiva. It is one of the twelve "Jyotirlingas" of Lord Shiva. Lying at an altitude of 3584 m at the head of river Mandakini, the shrine of Kedarnath is amongst the holiest pilgrimage for the Hindus. It is no wonder that Adiguru Shankaracharya–a great scholar and saint, chose to enshrine Lord Shiva in this land, where the unholy becomes holy and the holy becomes holier.

It is the place where Lord Shiva absolved Pandavas from the sin of killing their own cousins Kauravas in the battle of Kurukshetra. The origin of the revered temple can be found in the great epic Mahabharat.

At Kedarnath there are several Kunds (pools, tanks) that are known for their religious significance – Shivkund, Retkund, Hanskund, Udakkund, Rudhirkund are the most important. A little away from Kedarnath is a temple dedicated to Bhaironathji who is ceremoniously worshipped at the opening & closing of Kedarnath. The belief is that Bhairavnathji protects this land from evil during the time when temple of Kedarnath is closed.

During the winters, the shrine is submergd in snow and hence is closed. Fortunate are those who have good weather, but twice blessed are those who are Kedarnath on a moonlit night the snow peak gleams like hundred silver pinnacles atop the glittering mountains.

The holiest of Shiva's shrines is likened to gold among base metals so that every pilgrim finds peace here, and it is said that devotees who die here become one with Shiva himself. Beyond the temple is the highway to heaven, called Mahapanth. According to legend, the place came into being during the period when the five Pandava brothers were asked to seek Shiva's blessings, purging them of the sin of killing their cousins. Lord Shiva unwilling to give darshan to the Pandavas fled Kashi to live incognito in Guptkashi, where eventually he was detected by the Pandavas. While fleeing Shiva took refuge at Kedarnath in the form of a bull and started to plunge underground when he was spotted by the Pandavas. He dived into the ground, leaving behind his hump on the surface. No wonder the natural rock formation that is worshipped here resembles the hump of a bull. Thus, Shiva pleased with the determination of the Pandavas, exonerated them from their sin, gave them darshan and bestowed upon them the opportunity to worship his hump.

The other four places where Shiva is worshipped take their appearance from different parts of his body-the navel at Madmaheshwar, the arms at Tungnath, the face at Rudranath, and the matted hair at Kalpeshwar. The latter four along with Kedarnath are known as the Panch Kedars.

KEDARNATH TEMPLE

An imposing sight, standing in the middle of a wide plateau surrounded by lofty snow-covered peaks. The present temple, built in 8th century AD by Adi Guru Shankaracharya stands adjacent to the site of an ancient temple built by the Pandavas. It is constructed on a rectangular platform and built of extremely large and evenly cut grey slabs of stone. The exquisitely architectured temple is considered to be more than 100 years old. The inner walls are embellished with figures of deities and scenes from mythology. Outside the temple door a large statue of the Nandi Bull stands as guard. The temple has a Garbha Griha (inner sanctum where the idol is actually located) and a Mandap (area apt for assembly of pilgrims and visitors). In the centre of Garbha Griha there is conical rock formation, encircled by a narrow pradakshina path, which is

Kedarnath Temple

worshipped as Lord Shiva in his Sadashiva Form. There are many idols and small temples on the outer pradakshina path. Some of the large grey slabs bear inscriptions either in Pali or Brahmi but could not be deciphered to reveal any historical information. These inscriptions are of great archaeological importance as deciphering them can reveal very significant historical importance and answer the question of who exactly constructed the temple.

Puja timings are in the morning and evening. Morning puja is called Nirvana Darshan, when the Shiva pinda (conical rock) is worshipped in the natural form. Ghee and water are the main offerings. Evening puja is called Sringar Darshan when the Shiva pinda is adorned with flowers and ornaments. The pinda is graced with a golden umbrella suspended from above. The puja is accompanied to the chanting of mantras, chiming of bells overwhelming the gathering with a profound feeling of devotion. The divine blessings are also sought by performing important morning pujas like shubhprabhat, balbhog, shivapuja, astotar, rudrabhisek, mahabhishek and evening pujas like ekanta seva, ashtotar, shiv mahima, shiv namavali and sahasranam, *etc.* The pandas of Kedarnath are scholars of Sanskrit residing in the villages around Ukhimath and Guptkashi.

The opening date of Sri Kedarnath temple is fixed on the day of the Mahashivratri by the priests of Ukhimath temple which normally falls during the last week of April or the first week of May. The temple of Kedarnath opens 3-4 days before that of Sri Badrinath.

SHANKARACHARYA SAMADHI

The samadhi–the final resting place of Adi Guru Shankaracharya is located at the back of the Kedarnath Temple. The Adi Guru set up four dhams in four corners of India to revive Hinduism which has suffered a setback during the regime of Emperor Ashoka who had propagated Buddhism. It is believed, after establishing the four dhams in India, he went into his Samadhi at an early age of 32 years.

Shankaracharya Samadhi

GANDHI SAROVAR-CHOREBARI LAKE

A small lake (less than a km from the temple) from where Yudhisthir, the eldest of the five Pandavas, is believed to have departed to heaven. Floating ice on the crystal clear water of the lake fascinates the visitors. The access to the lake is through the moraines at the back of the temple of Kedarnath. It is referred as Gandhi Sarovar because Mahatma Gandhi's ashes were submerged in this lake.

VASUKITAL

Vasukital is a pearl set in an unrivalled natural setting. 6 km away from Kedarnath, at a height of 4135 m, the lake is surrounded by high mountains and offers an excellent view of the Chaukhamba peaks. The water is crystal clear and often seen with floating blocks of glistering ice. During winter

Vasukital

it is completely frozen. GMVN organises a 6 day Vasukital Trek during summer-Rishikesh-Gaurikund-Kedarnath-Vasukital-Gaurikund-Rishikesh.

GAURIKUND

It is the last motorhead, 5 km ahead of Sonprayag. The exotic trek to Kedarnath starts from here. As per religious texts, Goddess Parvati (another name Gauri) meditated here for a long time to win a consort in Lord Shiva. The Lord agreed and the cosmic couple were wed at Triyuginarayan.

GauriKund

An ancient temple dedicated to Goddess Gauri houses metallic idols of Gauri and Mahadev (Shiva). Near the temple are thermal springs of medicinal value. For trek to Kedarnath as it is advisable to travel light, lots of pilgrims make use of cloakroom facilities available here provided by Government Tourist Lodge and some private lodges.

Pilgrims usually stay here overnight to finalise all arrangements including engaging coolies, dandis and ponies.

SONPRAYAG

This is the place of confluence of Mandakini and Sone Ganga. The Mandakini flows from Kedarnath and the Sone Ganga comes from the Basuki Lake. The confluence with a superb mountain setting as back-drop acts like a magnet to force one to sit and contemplate the glory of nature.

The several years, Sonprayag was the last motorhead on Kedarnath route, now the road has gone ahead upto Gaurikund. For pilgrims to Triyuginarayan-the mythological venue of the marriage of Lord Shiva and Goddess Parvati, a 5 km black-topped motor road branches off from here.

GUPTKASHI

Perched at an altitude of 1479 m above sea level the town is known to be a place of hiding of Lord Shiva during the period when Shiva was unwilling to grant darshan to five Pandavas, who wanted emancipation from the curse of killing their own kinsmen in the epic battle of Mahabharat. The

Guptkashi

temples of Lord Vishwanath–the presiding deity of holy Varanasi and Ardhnarishwar are noteworthy. In front of this temple is a spring which local people believe that these are the waters coming from Gangotri and Yamunotri. From Guptkashi trips can be made to Kalimath and Madmaheshwar.

AGASTMUNI

This town is a little paradise with its deep blue murmuring Mandakini, lush green forests and terraced beds of green fields. The ideal place for relaxation and fishing on the banks of Mandakini. It is note worthy for the temple dedicated to the sage Agast who meditated here.

UKHIMATH

This is the winter seat of Lord Kedarnath and worship is done here during the winter when the temple of Kedarnath remains closed. The temples of Usha and Anniruddha (son of Lord Krishna), Shiva and Parvati are worth visiting. Ukhimath is at a distance of 41 km from Rudraprayag and 13 km from Guptkashi at an elevation of 1311 m. Ukhimath is connected by direct bus service with Rudraprayag, Gauri Kund, Guptkashi and Srinagar. From Ukhimath one can see on a clear day the beautiful view of the Kedarnath Peak, Chaukhamba and other green beautiful valley.

KALIMATH

It is situated close to Ukhimath, 23 km by bus and 10 km on foot. It is one of the Siddh Peeths of the region and held in high religious esteem. The temple of Goddess Kali located here is visited by a large number of devotees round the year and specially during the Navratras. The Peeth comprises temples made of wood and iron surrounded by several smaller ones made of stone, dedicated to different deities Mahalaxmi, Mahasaraswati, Gauri Shankar Mahadev and Bhairav. The goddess, who vanquished evil, is depicted beautifully along with the four-handed Shankar with Ganesh and Kartikeya placed at the feet of Gauri.

Kalimath

CHOPTA

27 km from Ukhimath and 40 km from Gopeshwar is one of the most captivating places in the entire Garhwal Himalayas. The wild forest and the awesome view of the Himalaya make it an amazing place to be in. Boarding lodging facilities are available at Dogalbitha about 8 km from Chopta.

TRIYUGINARAYAN

14 km (including 5 km trek) from Sonprayag at an altitude of 1980 m, this place is of great religious importance. Mythology has it that the wedding of Lord Shiva and Sati (Goddess Parvati) was solemnised here in the presence of Lord Vishnu. Of special interest is an eternal fire which according to legend believed never extinguishes. Kedarnath is 31 km from here. There is a Dharamshala and PWD Inspection House for overnight stay.

PANCH KEDAR (The other four Kedars)

Rudranath

The face of Shiva is worshipped here. The temple of Rudranath at 2,286 m, entails trekking through ridges at almost twice that height before reaching the meadow where it is located. Devotees come to Rudranath to offer ritual obeisance to their ancestors, for it is here, at Vaitarani river (the water of salvation), that the souls of the dead cross when changing world. It is 23 km from Gopeshwar, 5 km of the distance is motorable and the rest 18 km trek. The trek passes through wild orchards and picturesque bugyals and involves trekking over high ridges. The temple is surrounded by a number of pools – Surya Kund, Chandra Kund, Tara Kund, Manas Kund *etc.* – while the great peaks of Nanda Devi, Trishul and Nanda Ghunti rear overhead.

> Situated in the thick green wood, one of the panch kedars, Shiva is worshipped at Rudranath as Neel Kanta close to the temple, a few old rusted swords were found in the crevices of some rocks, believed to be those belonging to the Pandavas.

Rudranath

Anusuya Devi temple is located on the trek to Rudranath involving an additional trek of 3 km.

Kalpeshwar

> Located on the Bank of river Kalpeshwar, is the rock temple of Kalpanath - another name for Shiva. Another among the Panch Kedar, the temple of Kalpeshwar offers tourists and pilgrims a fascinating view of the nature.

It is the site where Shiva's hair appeared. A favourite spot for sages who come here to meditate, following the precedent of Arghya who performed austerities created the celebrated nymph, Urvashi, here, and the irascible Durvasa who meditated under the wish fulfilling tree, Kalpavriksha. Pilgrims pray at the small rock temple at the height of 2134 m before the matted tresses of Shiva enshrined in rock in the sanctum sanctorum. The sanctrum is preceded by a natural cave passage. Surrounded by thick forests and terraced fields in the Urgam valley, the temple is reached following a km long trek.

GMVN organises a 15 days Panch Kedar Trek in summer that includes all the five shrines associated with the legend-Rishikesh-Kedarnath-Madmaheshwar-Tungnath-Rudranath-Kalpeshwar-Rishikesh.

Kalpeshwar

Tungnath

> This Shiva temple's dome spans 16 doors housing an idol of Adi Guru Shankaracharya alongside the lingam. The Nanda Devi Temple is also situated at Tungnath. The awe inspiring Akashlinga waterfall so called because the water looks as though this descending from heaven, is nearby. During the month of winter, the priests move to Mukunath, 12 miles away from the Shiva Temple of Tungnath.

The arm of Shiva came out at this place as per Kedarnath myth. The Tungnath temple, at an altitude of 3680 m atop the Chandranath Parbat, 23 km from Ukhimath, is the highest Shiva shrine among the Panch Kedar. The sanctiy of the region of Tungnath is considered unsurpassed. The peak of Tungnath is the source of three springs that form the river Akashkamini. Tungnath is reached through a path that wends through alpine meadows & rhcododendron thickets. An hours' climb from here leads to Chandrashila with its panoramic views. The entire journey and the shine are located in some of the finest most picturesque pockets of the Himalayas.

Tungnath

Adding to the splendour are the spectacular Chaukhamba, Kedarnath and the Gangotri-Yamunotri peaks. GMVN organises 7 days round-the-year. Chandrashila Winter Summit Trek (except during heavy snowing months of December and January) the trek abounds in wildlife and offers a beautiful view of Nanda Devi, Trishul, Kedarpeak and Chaukhamba peaks Rishikesh-Ukhimath-Devaria Tal-Chopta-Tungnath-Chandrashila-Ukhimath-Rishikesh.

Madmaheshwar

It is said that, after disappearing at Kedarnath, the navel of Lord Shiva reappeared here at Madmaheshwar. Shiva is worshipped here in the form of a navel-shaped lingam. Located at the base of Chaukhamba peak, at an altitude of 3289 m the classic temple architecture belongs to the North-Indian style. So sanctified is the water here that even a few drops are considered sufficient for ablution. The natural scenery is dramatically wild, with deep gorges and valleys, mountain sides flung upwards towards the skies, the forests where the snow lies thick in winter, only to be replaced by a carpet of greenery in the summer. Kedarnath & Neelkanth peaks are visible from here, the entire ring of mountains associated with the life and times of Shiva. The confluence of Madmaheshwar Ganga and Markanga Ganga at Gaundar just short of the

Madmaheswar

The Shiva Temple near source of the Madmaheshwar river is the second Kedar. Administered by sole pujari and assisted by volunteers of Panwar family of village Gaundar, the temple's looked after by sole Pujari and assisted by the Kedarnath Trust. During the six months of winter only the shivling remains inside the temple whereas the silver idols are taken ceremonially to Ukhimath for worship. The place known as Saraswati Kund where parpanas are offered, is nearby.

temple, is one of the prettiest spots in the region. The best statue of Har Gauri in India, measuring over a metre high is found in the Kali temple.

BADRINATH

Badrinath Dham is one of the oldest of Hindu places of worship. On the right bank of the river Alaknanda lies the sacred shrine perched at an altitude of 3133 m above sea level, guarded on either side by the two mountain peaks Nar and Narain with the towering Neelkanth peak providing a splendid back-drop. Also known as the Vishal Badri, the largest among the five Badris, it is revered by all as the apt tribute to Lord Vishnu.

The revered spot was once carpeted with wild berries which gave in the name 'Badri Van' meaning 'forest of berries'. Built by Adi Shankaracharya, the philosopher-saint of the 8th century, the temple has been renovated several times due to damage by avalanches and restored in the 19th century by the royal houses of Scindia and Holkar. The main entrance gate is colourful & imposing popularly known as Singhdwar. References to Sri Badrinath have been made in the Vedas and perhaps it was a popular shrine during the Vedic age also. The Skand Purana gives an account of the Adiguru consecrating the idol of Lord Badri Vishal in the temple after recovering it from Narad Kund, in a pursuance of a divine call from heaven. The idol is made of black stone similar to granite. So holy is the shrine that it forms one of the four prominent places of Hindu worship. The epic Mahabharat, it is believed, was composed in the Vyas and Ganesh Caves close by. The Vishnu Ganga which later becomes the Alaknanda flows below the temple. Almost 3 km north of Badrinath, Mana is the last Indian village before the Tibetan border. The Vasundhara falls are quite spectacular. On the closing day, the residents of Mana offer a choli to the deity to cover the deity all the winter. It is taken off on the opening day and its fibres are distributed amongst the yatris as maha prasadam. Joshimath is the winter deity of Badrinath.

The temple opens every year in the month of April-May and closes for winters in the third week of November. Badrinath's four subsidiary Badris include Bhavishya Badri, Yogdham Badri, Bridha Badri and Adi Badri.

Badrinath is one of the Char Dhams of the country, also known as Vishal Badri, Vishnu Bhagwan is the other name of Lord Badri Vishal. It is popularly believed that with spread of Buddhism, the Buddhists enshrined the statue of Lord Buddha there and during the Hindu renaissance, the statue of Buddha was later restored by Adi Guru as the idol of Vishnu. This possibly explains the deity sitting in Padmasan posture, typical of Buddha icons. However, also 

Badrinath Mountain

according to Hindu mythology, Buddha was considered to be the ninth incarnation of Lord Vishnu.

Badrinath is devoted to the worship of Vishnu, who, according to an amusing tale, usurped this place from Shiva. For Vishnu had come here as the gods once did, to offer penance. He loved the place so much that he plotted to unseat Shiva from his meditation here. He took on the form of a beautiful child and began to wail. Shiva's wife, Parvati, picked him up but could not calm the child. Since his wailing continued to disturb Shiva, he shifted to Kedarnath in exasperation, leaving the spot free for Vishnu to occupy. But reminders of Shiva's stay continue to linger, most visibly in the name, Badri, a kind of berry that Shiva was most fond of and the gigantic tree, invisible to the mortal eye, that served Shiva. Legend also has it, when the Ganga was requested to descend to earth to help the suffering humanity, the earth was unable to withstand the force of its descent. Therefore, the mighty Ganga was split into twelve holy channels. Alaknanda was one of them that later became the abode of Lord Vishnu or Badrinath.

When the sage Narad disapproved of Lord Vishnu's way of living in worldly comforts, he was hurt and sent his spouse to nagkanyas. He himself decided to disappear in the Himalayan valley-whose peaks make for some of the most enticing manifestations of God's creations. The spot was carpeted with badris or wild berries and hence was famous as Badri Van. The Lord Vishnu assumed a yogdhyani posture and for several years meditated at the same spot and fed himself with wild berries. Laxmi on return found the sesha shayya empty, she went to the Himalayas in search of the Lord and ultimately found him amidst the badri in deep meditation. He addressed the Lord as Badrinath and requested him to give up the yogdhyani posture to return to his original sringaric form.

He agreed to do so provided the entire mankind abides by that he will be worshipped in yogdhyana form by the Gods and in sringaric form by the mortals and further Goddess Laxmi will sit on the left side in yogdhyani form and on right in sringaric form. The Hindu traditions demand that the place of the spouse is on the left but sitting of the Goddess Laxmi on the right is meaningful to convey that they should not be worshipped as a divine couple but as two individual deities with no marital relation. It is for this reason that the Rawal of Badrinath must not be married. The pilgrims to the temple worship the Lord in his sringaric form during the summer and in the winter, he is worshipped in his yogdhyani form by the devtas and sages. There are many sacred spots of pilgrimage in the heaven, earth but there has been none equal to Badri, nor shall there be.

The popular route is along the Alaknanda valley on the main road from Rishikesh to Badrinath. While going to Badrinath from Kedarnath, one has to return to Kund, where the road bifurcates into two, one via Rudraprayag and the other via Chopta to meet further on at Chamoli.

Airport: Jolly Grant, 317 km, Railhead: Rishikesh (300 km) and Kotdwar 327 km, *Road:* Badrinath is connected by a motorable road with Rishikesh, Kotdwar, Dehradun, Haridwar and other hill stations of Garhwal. Some important road distances are Delhi:- 518 km, Joshimath: 42 km, Haridwar 321 km; Gopeshwar: 106 km. Private Taxis and other vehicles are also available between Rishikesh and Badrinath. During season GMOU, TGMOU Temple Committee Buses operate from Rishikesh and Joshimath to Badrinath.

Gauchar is the area with vast flat land in the hills and air service from Dehradun and Delhi direct to this place is proposed 12 km from Gauchar is the place of confluence of river Pindar and Alaknanda at Karnaprayag – the name derived from popular hero of epic Mahabharat, Karna is believed to propitiate the Sun God here. There is also a temple dedicated to Goddess Uma Devi at the confluence of two rivers. Karnaprayag is the base for treks to Roopkund and Badni Bugyals and the approach to the Pindari Glacier 22 km from Karnaprayag, set amidst the scenic surroundings at the confluence of Mandakini and Alaknanda is Nandprayag 10 km from here is the town of Chamoli, on the banks of Alaknanda where the other route from Ukhimath meets. About 18 km away is Pipalkoti with ample facilities for night halt in dharamshalas, reasonable chattis and good eating places.

Garur Ganga further 5 km up is located on the banks of small rivulet taking its name from the carrier, Garur the eagle, of Lord Vishnu. It is believed than Lord Vishnu on his way to Badrinath left his carrier here to continue his journey to Badrivan on foot. The place also offers gorgeous view of the snow-clad peaks particularly the twin Hathi and Ghori Parvat. Helang 5 km further on way to Joshimath is approach to the temple of Kalpeshwar – one of the five Kedars. 14 km from Helang is the town of Joshimath the major halt en route Badrinath. It is the winter seat of Badrinath and the temple administration also. Through Vishnuprayag the meeting place of waters of Alaknanda and Dhauli Ganga, one reaches Govind Ghat which is base for the treks to the Valley of Flowers and the Sikh shrine of Hemkund Sahib. Pandukeshwar, 4 km from Govind Ghat, is believed to be the place from where the Pandavas proceeded to Swargarohan and their father king Pandu lived the last days of his life and attained nirvana.

10 km from Pandukeshwar at Hanumanchatti is a small temple of Hanumanji. It is believed that at this place, Hanumanji was blessed by Lord Badrinath with unusual powers and strength. The drive from Hanumanchatti is a continues steep climb through incredible sceneriy of rugged rocks, trailing waterfalls and with Alaknanda rushing down with gurgling sound one reaches dev darshani 13 km from where the first view of the temple is available.

Badrinath Temple

Dedicated to Lord Vishnu, it is built in the form of a cone with a small cupola of a gilt bull and spire. Legend dates the temple prior to the vedic age and the original temple is believed to be built by King Pururava and the icon of the lord carved by Vishwakarma, the creator of gods. A Hindu reformist Adi Shankaracharya re-enshrined the temple back in the 8th century. A flight of steps

Badrinath Temple

takes pilgrims to the main gate and then into the temple. The temple is divided into three parts – the 'Garbha Griha' or the sanctum sanctorum, the 'Darshan Mandap' where the rituals are conducted and the 'Sabha Mandap' where devotees assemble. The Garbha Griha portion has its canopy covered with a sheet of gold offered by Queen Ahilyabai Holkar. The complex has 15 idols. Especially attractive is the one-metre high image of Badrinath, finely sculpted in black stone. It represents Lord Vishnu seated in a meditative pose-Padmasan.

Special pujas are also performed on behalf of individuals. Every puja must be preceded by a holy dip in the Tapta Kund. Some of the special morning pujas are Abhishek, Mahaabhishek, Geeta Path. Some special evening pujas are Aarti and Geet Govind. Such pujas are to be booked in advance. The temple opens at 0430 hrs and closes at 1300 hrs. Once again it opens at 1600 hrs and closes at 2100 hrs after the divine song Geet Govind. Rawal is the administrator-Pujari of the temple well versed in puja ceremonials and Sanskrit language and is expected to be celibate. Nearby is a 'math' set up by Adi Shankaracharya.

The opening day of the temple is decided with a brief ceremony on the auspicious day of Basant Panchmi, which normally falls during last week of April or 1st week of May. Special significance is attached to the akhand jyoti darshan on the opening day. On the closing day, ghee and oil are put into the ancient lamp to make certain that it will continue to burn through out the year. The day of closing falls during the second week of November, which is finalised on the day of Dussehra. A woollen Choli, woven by young girls of the Molapa families of Mana, is offered to the deity as part of many ceremonies on the occasion of temple closing. Bhog is offered and mantras chanted. For the winter months the Lord will rest in the yogdhyan mudra and will only be worshipped by gods and Yakshas. The Choli, covering the deity all the winter, is taken off on the opening day and its fibres are distributed as mahaprasad to the pilgrims.

For the winter months everyone moves down to Joshimath and awaits the auspicious day for the temple to re-open. The Pujari of Badrinath is known as the Rawal who must be a Namboodripad Brahmin of Kerala. He is the religious head appointed by a temple committee and is assisted by a naib Rawal-also a Namboodripad Brahmin. The pandas of Badrinath hail from the town of Deoprayag 224 km away. These pandas play an important role in the rituals of the temple and act as guide to the pilgrims.

NARAD KUND

During the period when Buddhism dominated some fanatics threw the idol that was there in the Badrinath temple into the Narad Kund. It was in 8th century AD that Adi Guru retrieved the idol and he duly re-enshrined it. Narad Kund is a few yards from Tapt Kund. A dip in the kund is considered holy in a religious sense.

Narad Kund

TAPT KUND

It is the natural thermal springs on the bank of river Alaknanda, where it is customary to bath before entering the Badrinath temple. The water of the kund is believed to have medicinal properties. It is believed that after the holy bath, one's body is reinforced against the cold winds blowing off the icy waters of the river Alaknanda. The hot water springs come out from beneath the Garur Shila and fall into a tank and the constructed of stone and cement.

SHESNETRE

1.5 Km away on the opposite bank of the river Alaknanda, in the lap of Nar Parvat, there are two small seasonal lakes. Between these lakes is a boulder having an impression of the legendary snake, Sheshnag. The formation of eye on the boulder is natural.

NEELKANTH PEAK

At the back of the temple, a side valley opens to a conical shaped Neelkanth peak (6600 m.). It is popularly known as the Garhwal Queen. It is a shining pyramid of white crystals, which are ever ready to change their colour and hue. Reflecting the first glow of dawn into the valley and glittering like a golden temple, Neelkanth embodies all the divinity of this divine land.

Neelkanth Peak

BRAHMA KAPAL

In a quest to ensure a heavenly abode for the dead ancestors, the shradh ceremony (propitiating rites) or the offering of pind is an important part of Hindu rituals. After offering pind here, the spirits of the dead are permanently enshrined in Heaven and no more pinds are to be offered elsewhere. The Brahma Kapal, on the bank of the Alaknanda, is a flat platform a few yards north of the temple. Legend has it that when Shiva chopped of the fifth head of Brahma, it got stuck to his trident. Lastly, with the blessing of Lord Vishnu at Badrivan, the head of Brahma fell down from the trident at this place and hence the name Brahma-Kapal (head).

CHANDRAPADUKA

3 km away is a beautiful meadow carpeted with wild flowers in the summer. Here is a boulder bearing the footprints of Lord Vishnu. It is said that when Lord Vishnu descended from Vaikunth (the heavenly abode of Lord Vishnu) he stepped on this boulder. The area is a steep climb from the town and is full of caves and boulders.

PANCH DHARAS AND PANCH SHILAS

The Panch Dharas (five streams) which are famous in Badripuri are Prahlad, Kurma, Bhrigu, Urvasi and Indra dhara. The most striking of these is the Indra dhara, about 1.5 km north of the town Badripuri. Bhrigudhara flows past a number of the caves. The one on the right of river Rishi Ganga, originally from the Neelkanth range is Urvashi dhara. Kurma dhara, water is extremely cold whereas Prahlad dhara has lukewarm water, which glides majestically down the rocks of Narain Parvat. Around the Tapta Kund there are five blocks of mythological importance called Narad, Narshing, Barah, Garur and Markandey Shilas (stone).

Standing between Tapta and Narad Kund is conical formed Narad Shila. It is said that the sage Narad meditated on this rock for several years. Standing in the waters of Alaknanda just below the Narad Shila is a huge stone looking like a lion with its gaping jaws and hooked claws. It is said that Bhagwan Narshing after killing the demon king Hiranyakashyapa remained in the shape of a block of stone forever.

Near the Narad Kund the Barah Shila has the shape of boar. Barah is believed to an incarnation of Lord Vishnu.

The Garur Shila near the Tapta Kund had Garur (the carrier of Vishnu) fasted and medicated on this stone. Sage Markanday on the advice of Narad left Mathura to meditate here in Badrivan and attained ultimate peace. Markanday Shila is the stone on which the Sage meditated.

URVASHI TEMPLE

Legend has it that God Indra sent a group of beautiful celestial nymphs (apsaras) to distract Nar and Narain who were in deep meditation. Narain shattered the pride of Indra by tesing his left thigh from where several nymphs more attractive than them all appeared. He directed Urvashi to accompany these nymphs back to Indra. The temple dedicated to Urvashi has Narain holding a conch, chakra, a gada, a padma in his four hands with a celestial nymph seated on his left thigh. Named after Urvashi there is a small pond near Charanpaduka, where the pride of Indra was shattered.

MATA MURTI TEMPLE

On the right bank of Alaknanda opposite the Mana village is a small temple of Mata Murti dedicated to the mother of Sri Badrinathji. Once a year, on the day of Vamana Dwadashi, the Narain (Badrinathji) pays a visit to Mata Murti, when she is worshipped by the Rawal of Badrinathji and the residents of Mana village organise a festival of prayer, havan & bhog. Belief is that Mata Murti has the power of granting Vairagya to those who sincerely meditate here for a few days.

MANA VILLAGE

Inhabited by Indo-Mangolian tribe, it is considered to be the last Indian village before Tibet. The villagers of Mana are closely linked with the activities of Sri Badrinath temple for they offer a choli to the deity on the closing day of the temple – an annual traditional feat. The Mana village is full of caves and it is said that Ved Vyas dictated his famous epic of Mahabharat to Ganesh, in one of these caves, now known as Vyas Gufa (cave). Inside is a marble statue of Ved Vyas shown writing the granth (epic book). On this route a natural bridge over the Saraswati river and 122 m high Vasundhara falls form an important part of the pilgrimage to Badrinath.

The area around this remote village even in ancient times offered ideal setting and excellent shelter to philosophers and saints. The caves associated with ancient sages and yogis, like Ganesh Gufa, Bhima Gufa and Muchakanda Gufa are known since very long.

SARASWATI

3 km north of Mana village emerges the river Saraswati from a lateral glacier. Saraswati is known as the Goddess of learning, blessed Ved Vyas to compose the epic Mahabharata of Mana. The river after touching Vyas Gufa, gets lost in the Alaknanda at Keshav Prayag. From here to Allahabad, Saraswati flows incognito, that is why it is said that at the confluence of Ganga, Yamuna and Saraswati at Allahabad, the Saraswati remains invisible.

ALKA PURI

Via Mana village, 15 km from Sri Badrinath and 3 km from Laxmivan, lies the source of Alaknanda river from the glacier snouts of Bhagirath – Kharak and Sato panth glaciers. The place is supposed to be the abode of Kuber, Yakshas and Gandharvas. To the right of the Alkapuri Glacier at the base of the Balkenpeak, the Neelkanth and several other unnamed peaks can be seen. Further to the north, one can view the Chaukhamba peak in all its majesty.

SATOPATH LAKE

This triangular lake of serene waters has a perimeter of about half of kilometer & is situated at an elevation of 4402 m above sea level. Brahma, Vishnu and Maheshwar, the Hindu trinity, are believed to occupy one corner each of this lake.

On the day of Ekadashi, it is said that Lord Vishnu takes a holy bath in the lake and visit to Santopanth on those days is said to be most auspicious and rewarding. The trek to Santopanth is full of unexpected scenery and natural hazards. A good guide with arrangement of provisions like stove, cooked food, *etc.* is advisable.

BHIMPUL–BHIM'S BRIDGE

The bridge over the river Saraswati on the outskirts of Mana village is made of a huge slab of stone. It is believed that when the Pandavas and Draupadi were on their way to Swargashram, Bhim bridged the river with this huge slab to get them across. The view from the bridge is truly spectacular.

VASUNDHARA FALLS

3 km from Mana village, the Vasundhara falls, 125 m high, against the backdrop of snow covered mountains and glaciers is a captivating sight. The torrents of water come gushing down and are diffused in fine showers and soft mist by wind blowing from different directions. Close to the falls are prominent peaks of Satopanth, Chaukhamba and Balkum. One is also able to see the glacial snouts from where the river Alaknanda emerges.

Vasundhara Falls

GOVIND GHAT

It is the place of confluence of Alaknanda and Lakshaman Ganga river. It has an imposing Gurudwara named after Guru Govind Singh. About 15 km along to Ghangaria is the base for the treks to the Valley of Flowers and Hemkund Sahib.

SWARGAROHAN MOUNTAIN

Meaning ascent to Heaven–this fabled mountain is made up of seven steps of snow. Legend has it that Pandavas after visiting Badrinath, ascended to heaven by climbing this stairway. The route to Swargarohan is full of snowed glaciers and the trek should only been taken up with proper planning and adequate arrangements.

JOSHIMATH

An important town en route Sri Badrinathji has religious history, magnificent scenery, bracing climate and a hub of commercial centre all one needs for a holiday or a pilgrimage. Joshimath or Jyotirmath holds an important position in the history of Hindu revivalism. Adi Guru Shankaracharya got enlightenment here in a cave and in this cave he wrote his famous Shankar Bhasya. It is one of the four 'maths' organised by the Adi Guru, the other three being is Dwarika, Puri and Rameshwaram. Atop the cave is the Kalpvriksha, a mulberry tree that is said to be 2400 years old under which Adi Guru supposedly attained enlightenment.

Joshimath

In the evening the Shankaracharya of the 'math' delivers the holy parvachan (discourse).

Amongst the many temples of Joshimath, the most famous are the Narsingh and Durga temples. The statue of Narsingh Bhagwan is carved out of a Shaligram and is an exquisite work of art. It is generally believed that one arm of the statue is becoming thinner year by year, and ultimately, when Kalyug comes this arm will break. During Durga Puja pilthe grims throng Durga temple to worship from far away places.

At this temple, there is a tall statue of Vasudevji that was enshrined by the Adi Guru. As God Narsingh is an incarnation of Lord Vishnu, Lord Badrinath is worshipped in the Narsingh temple during the months of winter when temple of Badrinath is closed. Joshimath, thus becomes the winter home of Sri Badrinathji and this temple is situated on the slopes above the confluence of Alaknanda and Dhauliganga.

Joshimath is fast developing into a hill resort. A few miles above the town are the beautiful slopes of Auli and Gorson, which have developed into regular Ski resorts. An aerial ropeway links visitors from Joshimath to Auli and one can see the fabulous meadow of Auli and the glittering peaks of the Nanda Devi Sanctuary.

Joshimath is also the base for mountaineering expeditions to Trisul, Kamet, Dunagiri, Nanda Devi, Tolmahimal, Neelkanth, Devastan *etc.* and treks to Kauri pass complex, Valley of Flowers, Hemkund Sahib *etc.* It is here that plenty of accomodation choices are available. It is here at Joshimath that banking (travellers cheque encashment), market and medical facilities are available.

PANCH BADRIS (THE OTHER FOUR BADRIS)

Bhavishya Badri

Bhavishya Badri

The temple of Bhavishya Badri is at an elevation of 2744 m and is surrounded by dense forests. Located at Subain near Tapovan about 17 km east of Joshimath on Joshimath - Lata - Malari route, pilgrims have to trek beyond Tapovan, up the Dhauliganga river. Tapovan has sulphurous hot springs and the view of the Tapovan towards the north is simply breathtaking.

It is believed that when Kalyug comes the mountains Jay and Vijay at Patmila near Vishnuprayag will collapse, so making the present shrine of Badrinath inaccessible and Lord Badrinath will be worshipped here. Thus, the name Bhavishya Badri which literally means the Badri of the future. Bhavishya Badri is popular even now, enshrined here is a lion headed image of Narsingh.

Yogdhyan Badri

Yogdhyan Badri

The temple of Yog Dhyan Badri, one of the five Badris, is located at Pandukeshwar, just 24 km short of Badrinath on Rishikesh Badrinath highway. Located at an altitude of 1920 m named after the Pandava's king, the sanctum has an image of the lord in a meditative (Yodhyan) posture. The region surrounding the temple was known as Panchaldesh. It is the place where Pandu is believed to have married Kunti. According to the myth, the Pandavas, victorious after their battle against Kauravas, but emotionally scarred, came to Himalayas for penance and before seeking out the highway to heaven, handed over their capital Hastinapur to king Parikshit.

Bridha Badri

The temple of the Bridha (old) Badri is located at Animath, 7 km from Joshimath in the direction of Pipalkoti.

Before Badrinath was designated one of the four dhams the idol of Badrinath was worshipped here. It is said that when mankind entered the age of Kalyug, Vishnu chose to remove himself from the temple. Interestingly, the image was found by Adi Guru Shankaracharya at Narad Kund, and restored, though part of it remains damaged. The climb to the temple is through cultivated land and past Malta Groves. A very huge Banyan tree shelters the temple. Legend has it that the god Vishnu disguised as Bridh

Bridha Badri

(old) person, played with Ganeshji during period of his childhood.

Adi Badri

Another pilgrimage centre of importance in this group is of 16 temples almost 16 km from Karnaprayag on the Chaukhutia-Ranikhet road. The main temple is dedicated to Narayan and has raised platform in the pyramidal form where the idol is enshrined. Sculpted out of black stone, the idol of Lord Vishnu is a metre high. It is believed that these temples, dating back

Adi Badri

to the Gupta period, were sanctioned by Adi Shankaracharya. This place is situated quite far from the cluster of other four which form the Vishnu-Kshetra.

PANCHPRAYAG

Panchprayag confluence of the most sacred rivers, is considered the epitome of immortal piety. River confluences in India are considered very sacred, especially since rivers themselves are extolled as goddesses. And outside of Prayag, the great confluence of the Ganga, Yamuna and the mythical Saraswati at Allahabad, the most revered confluences are in Garhwal Himalayas, since the two mighty rivers Ganga and Yamuna and its tributaries trace their source to these mountains, the points at which they meet are sanctified as major pilgrimage centres. It is here that propitiatory and cleaning ceremonies are performed as part of the tenets of Hindu religion. Five prayags are Vishnuprayag, Nandprayag, Karnaprayag, Rudraprayag and Deoprayag.

Deoprayag

It is believed that a part of Vishnu's body lies here at Deoprayag. While the holy town of Gaya claims his feet, Deoprayag claims his navel.

Deoprayag is regarded as the most complete showcase of legends, heritage and traditions. 70 km from Rishikesh, here the Bhagirathi from Gaumukh and the Alaknanda from Satopanth unite and for most Indians, this confluence is no less holy than the Sangam at Allahabad. These three rivers flowing majestically through sculptured channels carved through the rocks have carved angular blocks of land around the confluence and the town is set into these

Deoprayag

three angles. Located at a height of only 618 m, Deoprayag is an invocation to the gods who have generously endowed this spot with tremendous natural beauty. It is believed that Lord Rama and his father King Dashratha did penance here. The temple of Raghunathji houses a tall image of Lord Rama made of black granite. The most celebrated event at Deoprayag is the congregation of devotees, who come here to worship at Raghunath temple. There is also a small temple popular as Bharat Mandir of Rishikesh in recluse. It is said that on fearing attack by Aurangzeb the pujaris from Rishikesh installed the same idol at Deoprayag as makeshift arrangement and later took it back to Rishikesh.

A big stone on the Bhagirathi's bank is called the Vashistkund named after sage Vashist, under whose auspices lord Indra performed his Yoga. The stone has the exact spot marked on it.

Rudraprayag

Named after Lord Shiva (Rudra), Rudraprayag is situated at the holy confluence of Alaknanda and Mandakini rivers, at a distance of 34 km from Srinagar. It is believed that to master the mysteries of music, the sage Narad worshipped Lord Shiva, who appeared in his Rudra incarnation to bless the sage. It was here, also, that Shiva's wife, Sati, was reborn

Rudraprayag

after her self-immolation because her father humiliated her husband. In her new life, as the daughter of Himalaya, she did penance here to ask the boon of Shiva as a husband once again. The ancient temple of Rudranathji is dedicated to Lord Shiva.

Rudraprayag is the point where the two roads branch off to the holy shrines of Kedarnath (84 km) and Badrinath (159 km).

The entire region is blessed with immense natual beauty, places of religious importance, lakes and glaciers.

50 years ago a blind Sadhu Swami Sachidanand worshipped here and was completely cured of his blindness, in gratitude he renovated the temple and built several necessary institutions at Rudraprayag.

Karnaprayag

Karnprayag

Situated 11 km from Gauchar, the icy flow from the Pindari Glacier becomes the Pindari river, and when it meets the Alaknanda at 788 m, the confluence is known as Karnaprayag. The wooded thickets of the hills surrounding Karnaprayag were the meeting ground for Shakuntala and Raja Dushyanta, immortalised in Kalidasa's immortal classic and a favourite ballad ever since. The place derives its name from Karna, the son of the Queen Kunti and her fiery lover, Lord Surya (Sun), Karna's lineage was kept a secret, but he propitiated the Sun God here, and acquired a pair of earrings and armour that made him invincible. Ultimately, he fell in the battle between the Pandavas and Kauravas, but remains a tragic hero for in life he never had the legitimacy he desired. The Karna Maudi is on the left bank of the river Hare Ganga first above the confluence of the Pindari and the Alaknanda. Two large stone images of Karna and his green Padmavati are installed here. The place is further sanctified owing to the belief that Ganga and Shiva also appeared here to Karna in person. Beside the temple dedicated to Karna, the temple dedicated to Goddess Umadevi, Narayan and Gopal stand at the confluence.

Karnaprayag is the base for treks to Roopkund and the Bedni Bugyals and the approach to the Pindari Glacier.

Nandprayag

Nandprayag

22 km from Karna Prayag, Nand Prayag at 914 m forms the confluence of the Alaknanda and Mandakini (flowing from a glacier near Nanda Devi Peak) rivers. On their way to Tapovan across Kunwari Pass or on their way to Roopkund, it is popular with trekkers. It is said that the confluence is named for the pious Raja Nanda. He came her to perform the Maha Yagna. The slab on which the Yagna was performed is

the foundation stone for the Nand temple. Nandprayag was once the capital of Yadu kingdom. It is also believed a dip in this confluence cleanses one of all the sins. According to one legend, the king had been promised the boon of Vishnu as a son. Unfortunately, the same boon had been granted to Devki, the imprisoned sister of the tyrant king, Kansa. Ultimately, the gods found an ingeneuos if wily solution: Vishnu would be born as Krishna to Devki but would be brought up by Raja Nanda's wife, Yasodha.

50 km north east of Nandprayag is Vairaskund where Ravana is believed to have done intense Tapasya to appease Lord Shiva and get his blessings. He offered as sacrifice his ten heads.

Vishnuprayag

One of the five prayags of the region, this place is situated at about 12 km from Joshimath.

Formed by the confluence of the impetuous Vishnu Ganga (known after this point, as the Alaknanda) and the Dhauliganga river, Vishnu Prayag, 1372 m, has an ancient temple called Vishnu Kund. It is said that the sage Narad worshipped Vishnu at this sanctified spot. The temple is associated with sage Narad's defiance of Lord Brahma. As a worshipper of Vishnu he defied Brahma, incurred his wrath and curse. It led to Narad's birth in human form and construction of the Vishnu temple. Visitors will find the

Vishnuprayag

Kagbhusandi Lake bewitching with its emerald green depths giving it a still surface, while on the banks, blossoms evoke the colours of nature in all her glory. The lake can also be approached from Vishnuprayag besides from Bhundhar village near Ghangaria.

❖__❖__❖

16 Famous Temples

HARIDWAR

The name Haridwar signifies the gateway to the God. Since this is the place where the pilgrimage to two famous temples–Kedarnath (Lord Shiva) and Badrinath (Lord Vishnu) is started. Haridwar is situated on the right side of the bank of the holy Ganga, and is the point where the river spreads over the northern plain. Haridwar is among the seven sacred cities of India. It is also one of the four venues for the Kumbha Mela, held in every twelve years. Haridwar has not only remained the abode of the weary in body, mind and spirit, but also served as a centre of attraction for many in learning the ancient arts, science and culture. Haridwar is long standing position as a great source of Ayurvedic medicines. There are many temples in Haridwar for the attraction of devout people. The famous temples are : Temple of Mayadevi, Daksheshwar Mahadeva temple, Tilbhandeshwar and Rameshwar Mahadeva Temple, Mahishasur Mardini Temple, Bilvakeshwar Mahadeva Temple, Pashupati Mahadeva Temple, Har Ki Pauri Temple, Ganga Temple.

There are another temples also. They are – Chandidevi Temple, Neeleshwar Mahadeva Temple, Gauri Shankar Temple, Anjanidevi Temple, Mansadevi

Haridwar's Temple

Ganga River

Temple, Shri Raghavendra Temple, Bharat Mata Temple, Kanch Temple, Gayatri Temple *etc.*

RISHIKESH

Bharat Temple: This temple is in Rishikesh. According to mythology, the younger brother of Lord Rama stayed here for sometimes.

Neelkantha Temple: This temple is situated at the distance of 12 km away from Rishikesh. It is at the height of 1,675 metres on a hill from sea level.

ALMORA

Almora, the historical capital of Kumaon can be reached from Delhi via Kathgodam and also Ramnagar. The following temples are worth to be seen in Almora.

Chitai Temple: This temple is situated at the distance of 4 km from Almora.

Jogeshwar Temple: This famous Lord Shiva Temple is at the distance of 34 km from Almora. This temple is situated in a valley surrounded by long trees of deodars. Nearabout 164 temples are situated together having archaeological importance which were constructed from time to time. These temples show the engraved sculpture of that time.

Baijnath Temple: This temple is situated in Almora district 41 km northside of Almora city. One group of temples is situated at the bank of Baijnath Sarovar. The beauty of these temples are very enchanting. These temples are of Shikhar style. This style is often found in Uttarakhand. At the left and right sides of Parvati statue, there are small statue of Shiva-Parvati, Laxmi-Narayan, Ganesha, Surya *etc.*

Baijnath Temple

The Sun Temple of Katarmal: This place is nearabout 9 miles west from Almora. We can go Kosi by bus from Almora. This distance is of 7 miles. After ascending the mountain we reach Katarmal. The famous Sun Temple of Uttarakhand is here. The main part of the temple is broken. The big statue of this temple is god Surya. The height of this temple is 3 feet 8 inches and width is 2 feet. God Surya is sat upon the seat of lotus. Decorated diadem is on the head of god Surya and there is a halo of the backside of the statue. This statue is made of brown stone. It is a creation of 12th century. The pavilion of this temple is very big. The statues of Shiva-Parvati, Laxmi-Narayan, Narsingh *etc.* are present here. The height of these statues is 8 feet and width is 3 feet. The doors of the temple are made of wood. On the doors, beautiful figures of gods and goddesses, animals and birds are engraved.

RANIKHET

Temples of Dwarahat: This place is at a distance of 12 miles north of Ranikhet. There are many temples here. The three groups of temples-Kachehari, Mania and Ratandeo are famous. The few temples have statues and others are empty. The fourth is Goojardeva temple which is excellent in artistic view. Around this temple, there are engraved stone-strips. On these strips, there are attractive figures of men and women in different postures. These are engraved in lively ways. Really, this temple is only one temple of its kind. But at present the lower part of this temple is remaining.

DEHRADUN

Lakhamandal Temple: This place is in Jaunpur sub-division (Paragana) of Dehradun district. We can go to Chakrata 58 miles away from Dehradun by bus and in the east of this place 22 miles away is Lakhamandal. This place is store of statues. It is believed that due to many statues, this place is called Lakhamandal. This place is

Lakhamandal Temple

situated near Yamuna river and the natural beauty of this place is unique.

There is only one old temple at Lakhamandal. This temple has unique feature of art. The statues of Shiva, Durga, Saptamatrika, Kuber, Laxmi-Narayan, Kartikeya, Surya *etc.* are collected here. There are two statues in human shape of 6th century outside of the temple. These statue are of Jay and Vijay with a staff in hand. There are statues of Ganga, Laxmi and Mahishmardini on the outer walls of the temple. Other statues are stored in a godown. The number of these statues are large and the time of these statues is from 5th century to 12th Century. There are some inscriptions in it.

Tapakeshwar Temple: This natural Lord Shiva Temple is made of rocks and caves. The water dips automatically from the rocks on naturally formed Shiva-Linga. Fairs are held at the time of Shivaratri here.

BADRINATH

Temple of Badrinath: This temple of Badrinath belongs to Vedic period. This temple was got constructed by Adi Shankaracharya in 8th century.

Maamurti Temple: This temple is the temple of Badrinath's mother.

KEDARNATH

Kedarnath Temple: This temple was got constructed by Adi Shankaracharya in 8th century. The Pandavas got constructed a temple at this place.

Bhairavanath Temple: There is a Bhairavanath temple outside the Kedarnath temple. Bhairavanath is considered to be the god of protection.

CHAMOLI

Trijugi Temple: It is believed that Lord Shiva was married to Parvati at this place. Intact flame is still burning which is supposed to be taken from the marriage kund.

Trijugi Temple

UTTARKASHI

Gangotri Temple: Gangotri is the source of the Ganga. It is believed that king Bhagirath meditated here for bringing of river Ganga on earth. This temple is made of rocks on the bank of river Ganga.

Yamunotri Temple: This temple was got constructed by the Queen of Jaipur at Yamunotri. It is not known who got it constructed first. The river Yamuna is worshipped here. Suryakund is near it.

17 Famous Religious, Historical and Tourist Spots

HARIDWAR

A gateway to heaven-Haridwar is indeed what its name signifies. Strategically located at the foothills of the Shivalik range, the place is one of the seven sacred cities of India. Haridwar is situated on the right bank of the sacred river Ganga.

In Hindu mythology Lord Vishnu is known as Hari and Shiva as Har, Dwar means gate, and it is for this reason that this place is known as Hardwar or Haridwar, as the gateway to the Four Shrines/Dhams of Uttarakhand. Mentioned as Mayapuri, Gangadwar, Mokshadwar in the ancient scriptures and epic, Haridwar always remained as a major Shaktipeeth for the devotees. God's footprints on the bank of holy river has given the town its sanctity and has left an indelible mark on the spiritual ethos of every Hindu. Haridwar is the point where the Ganga emerges from the

FAMOUS SPOTS AND TEMPLES

An ideal destination for wildlife and adventure lovers, Rajajee National Park (Chilla) is first 10 km from Haridwar. The park supports a wide variety of fauna with over 23 species of mammals, 180 bird species and 315 air fauna species. It is best known for its elephants. The places of interest include the religious focus of the town the main ghat, 1.5 km, Har-Ki-Pauri (the footsteps of God). This is the place where Lord Vishnu is believed to have left his footprint. The temple of Mansa Devi - one of the forms of Shakti (Durga) is accessible on foot (1.5 km) or through a ropeway (Udan Khatola). Chandi Devi Temple erected on Neel Parvat is believed to have the main statue installed by the Adi Guru Shankaracharya in 8th Century AD Daksha Mahadev Temple (4 km), Maya Devi Temple, Pawan Dham Temple (4 km), Lal Mata Temple (5 km). Bharat Mata Temple (5 km), Sapt Sarovar (6 km) are the other attractions dotting this holy city. For the comfortable darshan of the Maa Chandidevi and Maa Mansadevi, Udan Khatola is operational to cut short on time otherwise taken for the steep climbs.

Himalayas to begin its progress across the plains. Legend has it that the holy Ganga, the holiest of all rivers, which flows through this sacred city has actually been sanctified by the powerful Trinity of Hindu mythology. According to devotees Haridwar is one of the four places (other three being Ujjain, Nasik and Allahabad) upon which the Amrit (nectar) of immortality emerging out of the churning of ocean (samundra manthan) fell. This is manifested in two great events that take place at Haridwar-the memorable and the huge religious mela Kumbh Mela which happens once every 12 years and the Ardh Kumbh Mela, which comes once every six years.

Clock Tower in Haridwar

The footprints of Lord Vishnu are present on a slab of stone and it is said the Lord Vishnu blessed the gods with darshan at this place. This place continues to be the mystic venue for the purification of mind, body & soul.

The scenic beauty and the lush greenery, a unique Gurukul School of traditional education, the temples and the ghats, a number of dharamshalas (pilgrims shelters) all give the city a unique flavour and charm.

In the evening the ghats look breathtakingly beautiful, as thousands of diyas and marigold flowers float and illuminate the holy water of the Mother Ganga.

KALSI

This place is situated on the bank of Yamuna river in the northern part of Dehradun district. A written document of Ashoka is engraved on a slab of stone here. Its script is Brahmi and the language is Pali. Kalsi is such place of Uttarakhand where rock edicts are found. It seems that Kalsi was the famous centre at the time of Ashoka.

BADRINATH

It is a famous tourist centre and pilgrimage. It is in Uttarakhand and at the distance of 384 km from Haridwar. It is cradled in the mountain ranges of Nar-Narayan, with the splendid Neelkanth peak as the enchanting backdrop, is located the holiest of all the Hindu pilgrimages, Badrinath. Along the left bank of river Alaknanda the place is called Badrinath as it was once carpeted with 'badris' or wild berries.

KEDARNATH

Kedarnath is a famous tourist spot situated at the bank of Mandakini at the altitude of 11,750 feet in Chamoli district of the State. It is scenic spot situated against the backdrop of the majestic Kedarnath range. There is regular bus-services from Badrinath, Haridwar, Rishikesh, Dehradun for Kedarnath. The buses go upto Gaurikund. There is 14 km trek from Gaurikund.

Lord Shiva is considered the embodiment of all passions–love, hatred, fear, death and mysticism, which is expressed through his various forms. There are more than 200 shrines dedicated to Lord Shiva in Chamoli district itself, the most important one is Kedarnath.

GANGOTRI

Gangotri is situated at the height of 3140 metres from the sea level in Garhwal region of Uttarakhand. This place is surrounded by pine and deodar trees and free from pollution. This place is 19 km away from the place Gomukh. The 18th century shrine of Gangotri is believed to have been built by Gorkha General Amar Singh Thapa. The Gangotri temple is 20 ft high and made of white granite.

Gangotri Glacier

YAMUNOTRI

Yamunotri is primarily a place of religious pilgrimage. Hindus in large number visit the shrine of the goddess Yamuna here and bathe in the tank filled by hot springs. Devotees cook rice in one of the springs and then carry the consecrated rice back for those at home. The temple of Yamuna is main temple for worshipping here. This temple was got constructed in 19th century by the Queen of Jaipur-Gularia. In this century, the temple was destroyed by the glaciers two times. Due to this reason, it was re-constructed. There

Yamunotri

are many hot streams near the temple. The famous is Suryakund. Devotees cook rice or potato in this kund and use as 'prasad'. There is Divyashila near the temple and people worship Divyashila first and then worship Yamunotri.

NAINITAL

Nainital is perched at the height of 1938 metres in the central Himalayas of the Kumaon region lies picturesque Nainital. Its snow capped peaks, verdant valley, rolling meadows and crystal lakes have beckoned lovers of nature since ages. Nature has been generous in endowing Nainital with natural beauty that transcendents the ordinary and an abundance of flora and fauna. There are many lakes in Nainital. That is why it is called 'Lake District' of India. The most prominent lake is Naini Lake, ringed by the hills and named after the goddess Naini. A number of tourists visit Nainital throughout the year to explore its historic sites, wildlife reserve, fruit orchards, sanctified spots and the panoramic

Nainital

environs that very few hill station of India can equal. Uttaranchal High Court is situated at Nainital. It is an important administrative hub for the Kumaon region.

Places worth visiting in Nainital proper are the Naina Peak, snow view, High Altitude Zoo, Khurpatal, Kilbury, Lands End, Kainchi Temple, Hanumangarhi and the State Observatory. The attractive destinations in the district include Bhowali, Golla Devta, Jeolikote, Ramgarh, Mukteshwar, Sat-tal, Bhimtal, Naukuchiatal, Ramnagar, Corbett National Park, Kaladhungi, Corbett waterfalls and the Garjia Temple.

Almora, the historic capital of Kumaon can be reached from Delhi via Kathgodam and also Ramnagar. It is 50 km away from Ranikhet. This town seems to be astride a horse. In 1563, King Kalyan Chand founded Almora. In the 17th century, the Capital of the Chand rulers was shifted from Champawat to Almora. For years, Almora housed the headquarters of the Chand kings, Gorkha invaders and the British. Two rivers– Kausik (Kushi) and Shalmali flow in its two sides.

Almora

There is a place namely 'Bright and Corner' which is 2 km away from Almora. From here, the unique scenic beauty of sunset and sunrise can be seen from here. Chitai Temple is situated at the distance of 4 km from Almora. In the temple, the statue of Devgol deity is present who was the brave army commander of Chand kings. He is worshipped later on as a deity. At the distance of 3 km there is Deer Park which is a good place for wandering.

The other place which are worth seeing include–Kasar Devi, Kausani, Katarmal, Bageshwar Baijnath, Pindari Glacier, Binsar, Gananath, Lakhudiyar, Jageshwar, Mritola Ashram, Chaubatia, Bhaludham, Jhoola Devi Ram Mandir, Mankameshwar, Upat and Kalika, Hairakhan Temple, Tarikhet Binsar, Mahadev, Majkhali, Dwarahat, Chaukhutia, Bhikhiasain, Manila etc.

There is a famous Jogeshwar Temple of Lord Shiva which is 34 km away from Almora. This temple is surrounded by Deodar trees from all side and situated in a valley.

RANIKHET

Ranikhet

Ranikhet is located at the distance of 59.5 km from Nainital. Ranikhet with its majestic pine trees amidst the rustling and encircled by dazzling white peaks, glistening in the sun, once camped a beauteous queen of legend and lore, giving the town its name–Rani (Queen)-khet (field) falling in love–with the beauty of the place. She decided to stay and built a palace near what is now the Ranikhet Club.

There is a place named Chaubatia where four ways meet. That is why, it is called Chaubatia. There are many fruit gardens and beautiful flower gardens. Different kinds of fruits are available here in every season. There is a Government Fruit Research Centre complete with a fruit sales depot and cafeteria.

At the distance of 35 km, there is Sheetalaghat. This place is completely secluded place. Wild animals can be seen here. This place is surrounded by verdant forests from all sides. This place is suitable picnic spot. There is Juladevi temple away from 7 km from Ranikhet. This place lies in the way of Chaubatia. The famous temples of Durga and Ram are here. It attracts the attention of people forcibly. Bhaludam is situated 3 km ahead from Chaubatia. It is also a suitable picnic spot. An artificial lake has been constructed here. Bhaludam is main source of town's water supply. It is famous for its fishing.

KAUSANI

Kausani is situated at the distance of 32 km from Almora. Bus and taxi services are available to reach here from Almora. There is also direct bus service from Nainital also. Kausani is the most attractive place of Uttarakhand. This place is situated on high hills surrounded by forests. This

Kausani

picnic spot is really very attractive and it is called 'Switzerland of India'. The scenic view of sunset and sunrise can be seen from here which are very attractive. The main attraction of Kausani is its natural beauty. The tourists visit this place and enjoy high dense forests and its scenic beauty.

MUSSOURIE

Mussourie is one of the most popular hill stations of India. It is called the Queen of the Hills. Mussourie's fame lies in its great scenic beauty, gay social life and great hotels. It is at the height of 2,005 metres from the sea-level and stretched in the area of 65 square km. Gun Hill is a high peak. It offers a beautiful panoramic view of the Himalayan ranges namely Bunderpunch, Srikanta, Pithwara and the Gangotri groups *etc.* At the time of the British Government, there was a gun which was shot daily to tell the time of 12 O'clock. Due to this reason this hill is called 'Gun Hill'.

Mussourie

Mussourie offers for sale wooden objects, Garhwal textile, woollen and richly embroidered Garhwali dresses. The main shopping areas are the Mall, Kulri Bazar and Landour Bazar.

The other places of attraction in Mussourie are Kempty Falls, Municipal Garden, Camel Back Road, Jharipani Fall, Bhatta Fall, Mossey Fall, Nag Devta Temple, Mussourie Lake, Sir George Everest House and Dhanolti.

DEHRADUN

Dehradun is a beautiful city situated at the height of 709 metres above the sea level at the foothills of Shivalik. It is also the temporary Capital of Uttarakhand State. Surrounded by lush green forests and hills, Dehradun has always been a favourite with the tourists. It is endowed with a pleasant, moderate climate and is well-connected to other important places.

Dehradun has an attractive tourist destination appreciated as much for its beautiful setting as for its mild climate and leisure opportunities. The most important town of Uttarakhand, it also serves as the gateway to Mussourie, the Queen of the Hills. The city lies in the verdant Doon Valley on the watershed of the Ganga river. In 7th century, it was a part of Garhwal State. In 1814, it was taken by the Britishers in their control. This place attracted the English very much. That is why, they developed it as a grand tourist spot.

INSTITUTES

Recorded at the best centre on Himalayas Geology, the **Wadia Institute of Himalayan Geology** maintains a museum displaying the geological diversity of the sub-continent. **Forest Research Institute (FRI)** is undoubtedly one of the finest institute of forest services recognised globally maintaining six museums, covering various disciplines in forest maintenance and management. Founded in 1767, the **Survey of India** has its headquarter, four kms off Rajpur road. The Surveyor Generals of this premier institute included Sir George Everest.

TEMPLES & OTHER SPOTS

Located in the cantonment area in Garhi, 5 kms from Dehradun city, is **Tapkeshwar Temple** dedicated to Lord Shiva. A remarkable feature of this cave temple is the natural formation of two Shivlings- including the one Dronacharya worshipped. It is beside a stream, which when flowing is directed onto the Lingam. 14 km from Dehradun, noted for its natural beauty and medicinal properties. **Sahastradhara** is a very popular picnic and entertainment spot. 43 km from Dehradun, on Dehradun-Chandigarh-Shimla highway is water sports resort **Assan Barrage.** 14 km from Assan Barrage is **Dakpathar**, an aquatic complex with a swimming pool, located at the foothills of Shivalik hills on the banks of river Yamuna. 16 km from

Tapkeshwar Temple

Dakpathar across the Yamuna river is **Paonta Sahib**-the Gurudwara of Guru Gobind Singh Ji. Once a cantonment town in British India, at an altitude of 2118 m, 92 km from Dehradun and 73 km from Mussourie. **Chakrata** is a place blessed with natural beauty. Virgin forest of conifers, rhododendrons and oaks are best suited for long walks. **Chakrata is restricted for**

Chakrata

foreign tourists. Prior permission of competent authority is essential. The deity of Mahasu is worshipped in the village of Hanol, 188 km from Dehradun, on the eastern bank of Tamas (Tons). It is located at an altitude of 1492 m.

The place has numerous picnic spots as also places to see. These include the historic Indian Military Academy, the Forest Research Institute, Wildlife Institute of India, and numerous other scientific institutions of repute. The city is also home to some of the most famous schools of Asia and is also called the school-city. The interesting places to visit include Lacchivala, Lakshamansidha, Guru Ram Rai Darbar, Rajaji National Park, Mussourie Lake etc.

RISHIKESH

At a distance of 22 km from Haridwar, surrounded by Shivalik hills of the Himalayas on three sides, Rishikesh is known as the World Capital of Yoga. Rishikesh is the base for Char Dham Yatra and gateway to Garhwal Himalayas, Sikh shrine of Hemkund Sahib and Valley of Flowers.

For the devout Hindu, however, the seat of meditation is Rishikesh, the place where the Ganges meanders out of the hills and enters the plains. Compared to Haridwar, Rishikesh is more tranquil and offers some of the best meditation spots. The place derives its name from the legend of Raibhya Rishi, who is said to have been

Laxman Jhula Temple

rewarded by a visitation from God for his undying devotion and austere penance. A number of ashrams (hermitages) offer Yoga and meditation courses for those in quest of spiritual fulfillment. Some come to Rishikesh to learn the ways of the mystics while others come here to discover their inner selves. Most of the ashrams have arrangement for fooding and lodging.

The Ganga has two suspension bridges–Lakshman Jhoola on the way to Badrinath and Ram Jhoola between Sivananda Ashrams and Swargashram. NE along the Ganga river is somewhat secluded sandy area Muni-ki-Reti (sand of the sages) is the area along the Chandrabhaga river having some temples

40 km from the town of Dehradun, this gorge centered town has acquired significance for being the centre for white River Rafting, Trekking and mountaineering. For the adventurous lot it is the starting point of many expeditions towards Himalayan peaks and for Skiing at Auli. It has recently developed to be an important centre for treatment-using the ancient methods of treatment nature and ayurved-for difficult to treat ailments and stress-induced problems.

PLACES OF INTEREST AND TEMPLES

Places of interest includes **Triveni Ghat,** believed to be the confluence of river Ganga, Yamuna and Saraswati is the most important religious spot for rituals. The aarti ceremony accompanied with chanting of religious hymns offers a spectacular sight. The suspension bridge **Lakshman Jhoola,** 5 km from Rishikesh on the way to Badrinath is on the west bank of Ganga. **Bharat Mandir,**

Bharat Mandir

named after Lord Rama's loyal brother is dedicated to Lord Vishnu Situated at an elevation of 1550 m is the temple of **Neelkanth Mahadev**-the place where Shiva is believed to have consumed poison churned out of the ocean.

> *The prominent spiritual institutions — the seats of spiritual learning include Sivanand Ashram (Divine Ashram Society) Parmarth Niketan Ashram, Swargashram, Omkaranand Ashram, Geeta Bhawan, Vithal Ashram, Yog Niketan, Kailash Ashram.*

Parmarth Niketan Ganga Aarti

ॐ जय गंगे माता, मैया जय गंगे माता।
जो नर तुमको ध्याता, जो नर मैया जी को ध्याता।
मनवांछित फल पाता, ॐ जय गंगे माता।

Om Jaya Gange mātā, Maiyā jaya Gange mātā
Jo nara tumako dhyāta, Jo nara maiyā ji ko dhyāta
Manavānchhita phala pātā, Om Jaya Gange mātā,

Hail to you, O Mother Gangā, the river goddess,
your worshipper gets all his desires fulfilled

चन्द्र—सी ज्योति तुम्हारी, जल निर्मल आता,
मैया जल निर्मल आता, शरण पड़े जो तेरी,
सो नर तर जाता, ॐ जय गंगे माता"

Chandra si jyoti tum hari, Jala nirmala ātā,
Maiya jala nirmala ātā, Sharana pade jo teri,
So nara tara jātā, Om Jaya Gange mātā

You are glorious like the moon with clear water,
Whoever surrenders himself to you gets beyond all difficulties.

पुत्र सागर के तारे, सब जग को ज्ञाता,
मैया सब जग को ज्ञाता, कृपा दृष्टि तुम्हारी,
दया दृष्टि तुम्हारी, त्रिभुवन सुख दाता,
ॐ जय गंगे माता"

Putra Sagara Ke tāre, Saba jaga ko gyāta
Māiyā saba jaga ko gyāta, Kripa drishti tumhāri,
Daya drishti tumhāri, Tribhuvana sukhadātā,
Om Jaya Gange mātā

The whole world knows that you redeemed the sons of King Sagar.
Your kind eyes are the giver of happiness to the three worlds.

एक ही बार जो तेरी, शरणागति आता
मैया शरणागति आता, यम की त्रास मिटाकर,
यम के कष्ट मिटाकर, परम गति पाता, ॐ जय गंगे माता

Eka hi bāra jo teri, Sharangati Ā tā
Māiyā Sharanagati Ā tā, Yama ki trāsa mitākara,
Yama ke kashta mitākara, Param gati pātā
Om Jaya Gange mātā,

One who comes to your shelter is saved the agony of death and is a
liberated from the wheel of death and birth.

मंगल कारिणि मैया, तू है सुखदाता

मैया तू है सुख दाता, तेरी गोद में आकर,

तेरी शरण में आकर, मन शान्ति पाता, ॐ जय गंगे माता

Mangal kārini maiyā, Tu hai sukhadātā
Maiyā tu hai sukhdātā, Teri godha men ākar,
Teri saran men ākar, Mana shānti pātā,
Om Jaya Gange mātā.

You are the holy Mother, giver of all happiness
In your lap, the mind attains peace.

ब्रह्म स्वरूपिणि मैया, जो तुमको ध्याता

मैया जो तुमको ध्याता, तेरी दया से सो जन

तेरी कृपा से सो जन, सद्गति है पाता, ॐ जय गंगे माता

Brahma Swarūpini maiyā, Jo tumko dhyātā
Maiyā Jo tumko dhyātā, Teri dayā se so jana
Teri kripā se so jana, Sadgati hai pātā
Om Jaya Gange mātā.

You are verily the Brahman.
O Mother, your devotees, by the virtue of your graciousness find
the right path in life and life beyond

आरति मात तुम्हारी, जो जन नित गाता

मैया प्रेम सहित गाता, दास वही है सहज में

भक्त वही है सहज में, मुक्ति को पाता, ॐ जय गंगे माता

Ā rati māta tumhāri, Jo jana nita gātā
Maiyā prema sahita gātā, Dāsa vahi hai sahaj men
Bhakta vahi hai sahaj men, Mukti ko pātā

One who chants your name regularly is relieved of
misery and gets liberated.

LANSDOWNE

This place is 45 km away from Kotdwar. Here is a big cantonment. The beauty of snow covered Badrinath mountain range is very attractive. The forests of deodar and baloots are very attractive for tourists.

PINDARI GLACIER

Pindari Glacier

This beautiful spot is in Almora district at the height of 3943 metres. The river Pindari flows from here. This glacier is near the Nanda Khat and other lofty peaks. Its access is very easy. Close to the Pindari glacier, there is an open meadow and lofty moraine made of gravel, mud and blocks of snow. The trek to glacier starts from Kapkote, which is last bus terminus. The trekking route is passing through waterfalls, pine forests, meadows and having magnificent views of the peaks.

RELIGIOUS AND TOURIST SPOTS

Religious Centres: Kedarnath, Badrinath, Gangotri, Yamunotri, Haridwar and Rishikesh.

Hilly Centres: Nainital, Ranikhet, Mussourie, Almora, Pithoragarh, Pauri, Lansdowne.

New Centre: Bhimtal, Kausani, Dak Patthar (Nainital).

Religious and Tourist Spots of Uttarakhand
AT A GLANCE

- ❖ **Almora:** Grand and traditional temples of goddess Kaushikidevi on Kashyap hill.
- ❖ **Badrinath (Chamoli):** One of the famous places of worship, situated at the distance of 384 km from Haridwar, the famous places which lie in the bus route from Rishikesh are Muni-ki-Reti, Devprayag and Kirtinagar, Kotdwar, Pauri, Srinagar, Rudraprayag, Karnaprayag, Nandaprayag, Chamoli and Peepal Kothi.
- ❖ **Baijnath (Almora):** Situated in the north side, 64 km away from Almora, group of temples at Baijnath Sarovar.
- ❖ **Chakrata (Dehradun):** Peaceful and invigorating place and we can see the snow capped crest here.
- ❖ **Corbett National Park (Nainital):** Famous for natural beauty and wild animals.
- ❖ **Gangotri (Uttarkashi):** Gomukh, present source of river Ganga, Gangotri Temple, Bhagirathi Temple *etc.*

- ❖ **Haridwar:** Famous as Mayapuri or Mayakshetra in Sanskrit literature, various temple, special importance of bath at Har-Ki-Pauri.

- ❖ **Kankhal (Haridwar):** Dasheshwar Mahadev Temple, Temple of Hanuman.

- ❖ **Kanvashram (Garhwal):** Present name Chaukighat, the area from Kanvashram to Nandagiri is thought to be provider of worldly pleasure and deliverance.

- ❖ **Katarmal (Almora):** The Surya Temple of 12th century.

- ❖ **Kedarnath (Chamoli):** Situated at the distance of 400 km from Haridwar, the famous temple of Kedarnath situated at the height of 11,500 feet above the sea-level.

- ❖ **Lakhamandal (Dehradun):** 128 km away from Dehradun, nearabout lakhs of temples are found on the banks of Yamuna. That is why named Lakhamandal.

- ❖ **Lansdowne (Pauri-Garhwal):** 45 km away from Kotdwar, worth visiting place of Badrinath snow capped crest.

- ❖ **Mussourie (Dehradun):** 35 km away from Dehradun, situated at the height of 6,500 feet, Queen of the Hills, Lal Bahadur Shastri Academy of Administration is situated.

- ❖ **Nainital:** surrounded by hills from three sides, famous attractions of Nainital are–Sat-tal, Bhimtal, Naukuchia tal, Khurpatal tal, etc.

- ❖ **Nanda Devi (Chamoli):** Highest peak of the world after Gaurishankar, religious congregation on every twelfth year on Bhadra Sudi Saptami.

- ❖ **Pindari (Glacier):** Situated at the height of 3,943 metres, attractive snow capped place elegant forest, source of Pinder river.

- ❖ **Purnagiri (Nainital):** Famous monastery where famous statue of Deviji is situated, fair in the Hindi month of Chaitra.

- ❖ **Rajajee National Park (Chilla):** Wildlife Sanctuary.

- ❖ **Ranikhet (Almora):** Forests of pines and many gardens of flowers, famous Golf-Course.

- ❖ **Rishikesh (Haridwar):** Attractive place and Pilgrimage, a number of temples are situated here.

- ❖ **Tapovan (Tehri-Garhwal):** Meditative place of Laxmanji, Laxman Temple, Laxman Jhoola, Swargashram is situated at the bank of river Ganga.

❖ **Valley of Flowers (Chamoli):** In 'Skandhapuran' known as Nandan Kanan, at the border of Myundar village at the height of 12,000 feet. The Valley of Flowers is surrounded by walls of snow ranges and a courtyard in the middle.

❖ **Yamunotri (Uttarkashi):** Hot water stream near Yamuna Temple, Divyashila near Suryakund, Water egression regions of Hanuman Ganga and Tonse rivers.

MAIN CITIES OF UTTARAKHAND

Almora	Haridwar	Nagla
Badrinathpuri	Jaspur	Nainital
Bageshwar	Jhabrera	Nand Prayag
Banbasa	Joshimath	Narendra Nagar
Bandia	Kachnal Gosain	Pauri Garhwal
Barkot	Kaladungi	Pithoragarh
Bhimtal	Karn Prayag	Ramnagar - Nainital
Bhowali	Kashipur	Ranikhet
Daman and Diu	Kashirampur	Roorkee
Chamba - Tehri Garhwal	Kedarnath	Rudra Prayag
Chamoli Gopeshwar	Kela Khera	Rudrapur - Udham Singh Nagar
Dehradun	Khatima	Shaktigarh
Dev Prayag - Pauri Garhwal	Kichha	Sitarganj
Dev Prayag - Tehri Garhwal	Kirtinagar	Srinagar - Pauri Garhwal
Dhaluwala	Kotdwara	Sultanpur-Udham Singh Nagar
Dhandera	Laksar	Tanakpur
Dharchula	Lalkuan	Tehri Garhwal
Dharchula Dehat	Landaura	Udham Singh Nagar
Didihat	Lansdowne	Uttarkashi
Dineshpur	Lohaghat	Corbett National Park
Dogadda	Mahua Dabra Haripura	Mukteshwar
Dwarahat	Mahua Kheraganj	Mussourie
Gadarpur	Manglaur	Pantnagar
Gangotri	Mohanpur Mohammadpur	Rishikesh
Gochar	Muni-Ki-Reti	
Haldwani-cum-Kathgodam		

❖__❖__❖

18

Famous Fairs and Festivals

FAMOUS FAIRS OF UTTARAKHAND

Many fairs are held every year in Uttarakhand. The description of some fairs is given as under:

FAIRS HELD FOR TOURISTS' ENTERTAINMENT

- **Shree Govardhan Pooja:** This pooja is organised to remember the events related to Lord Krishna in the most part of Uttarakhand.

- **Grismotsava (Almora):** To attract tourists in Summer, many programmes are organised in Almora.

- **Sharadotsava:** To attract tourists, Sharadotsava is organised in Almora, Mussourie, Ranikhet, Pithoragarh, Chamoli *etc.* places.

- **Surkhanda Utsav (Tehri-Garhwal):** This utsav is organised at the time of Surkhanda Devi worship in Tehri-Garhwal.

OTHER FAMOUS FAIRS

- **Bala Sundari Fair (Kashipur):** This fair is held at Kashipur for ten days beginning from Chaitra ashtami of Shuklapaksh. Goddess Parvati is worshipped in this fair and newly wedded couples come here to worship the goddess for happy married life.

- **Nanda Devi (Nainital):** These two are held at the time of winter solstice and summer solstice for the worship of Nanda Devi. These fairs are held in Almora in which enchanting and rare tableaus of folk culture are presented for three days.

Nanda Devi Fair

- **Peeraan Kaliyar (Roorkee):** This fair is held at the time of urs of Hazrat Sahib in which Hindu and Muslim both take part and worship.

- **Devi Dhura Fair (Pithoragarh):** This wonderful fair is held at every Purnamasi. In which people throw stones at one another. After that the priest makes compromise among them.
- **Jaljeeva Fair (Pithoragarh):** It is a professional fair. It is organised in Pithoragarh-district at Jaljeeva.
- **Maneshwar Fair (Pithoragarh):** On the occasion of this fair, a wonderful stone namely Maneshwar is worshipped.
- **Fair of Tapeshwar Siddh (Dehradun):** This fair is organised on the occasion of Shivaratri in Tapeshwar Siddh Temple.
- **Jhanda Fair (Dehradun):** This yearly fair is the fair of the Sikh and the followers of other religions. In which a flag made of special kind of bamboos is worshipped.
- **Kumbha and Half Kumbha:** From time immemorial in India, there are four religious cities–Haridwar, Prayag, Ujjain and Nasik where Kumbha, Half Kumbha and Sinhastha Kumbha are held. These Kumbha fairs attract the faithful Indians. The traditional Kumbha fairs of India in which one place of Kumbha lies in Uttarakhand. Not only Kumbha but also half Kumbha is also held in this city of Uttarakhand. After third year of Haridwar Kumbha, the Kumbha of Prayag comes and after three years, the half

Kumbha Fair

Kumbha of Haridwar comes. The Kumbha of Haridwar attracts people in a very large number. It has scientific, social and religious importance. Haridwar is situated on the right side of the bank of the holy Ganga, and is the point where the river spreads over the northern plains. Associated with both Lord Shiva and Lord Vishnu. Haridwar is among the seven sacred cities of India. It is also one of the four venues for the Kumbha Mela, held in its magnitude every twelve years.
- **Punyagiri Mela (Janakpur):** This place is situated 24 km away from Janakpur. It is in Pithoragarh district and largest fair of Kumaon region held in month of March and October. Punyagiri Shaktipeeth situated on the top of a mountain on the right bank of the river Kali is the site for many fairs. The temple is very crowded during the Navratris. Punyagiri fair is held in the Hindu months of Ashwin and Chaitra corresponding to the months of March-April and September-October respectively. The Punyagiri fair starting from Vishuwat-Sankranti is the largest fair of Kumaon, lasting for about 40 days.

Different festivals are celebrated by the different communities of Uttarakhand. The festivals which are celebrated by the Hindu community are given as under:

	Festivals	Time
1.	Samvatsarambha	Chaitra Shukla Pratipada
2.	Ram Navami	Chaitra Shukla Navami
3.	Hanuman Jayanti	Chaitra Shukla Purnima
4.	Sheetala Ashtami	Vaishakha Krishna Ashtami
5.	Vat Savitri Vrata	Jyeshta Krishna Trayodashi
6.	Ganga Dussehra	Jyeshta Shukla Dashami
7.	Nirjala Ekadashi	Jyeshta Shukla Ekadashi
8.	Kabir Jayanti	Jyeshta Shukla Purnima
9.	Hariyali Teej	Shravan Shukla Tritiya
10.	Nagpanchami	Shravan Shukla Panchami
11.	Tulsi Jayanti	Shravan Shukla Saptami
12.	Raksha Bandhan	Shravan Shukla Purnima
13.	Hal Shashti	Bhadrapad Krishna Shashti
14.	Janmashtami	Bhadrapad Krishna Ashtami
15.	Ganesh Chaturthi	Bhadrapad Shukla Chaturthi
16.	Radha Ashtami	Bhadrapad Shukla Ashtami
17.	Ananta Chaturdashi	Bhadrapada Shukla Chaturdashi
18.	Pitri Visarjan Amavasya	Ashwin (Kwar) Krishna-Amavasya
19.	Navratra (Begins)	Ashwin Shukla Pratipada
20.	Durga Navami	Ashwin Shukla Navami
21.	Vijaya Dashami	Ashwin Shukla Dashami
22.	Sharad Purnima	Ashwin Shukla Purnima
23.	Karva Chaturthi	Kartik Krishna Chaturthi
24.	Ahoi Ashtami	Kartik Krishna Ashtami
25.	Dhan Teras	Kartik Krishna Trayodashi
26.	Narak Chaudas	Kartik Krishna Chaturdashi
27.	Deepawali	Kartik Krishna Amawasya
28.	Annakoot	Kartik Shukla Pratipada
29.	Bhai Dooj	Kartik Shukla Dwitiya
30.	Devotthan Ekadashi	Kartik Shukla Ekadashi
31.	Kartik Purnima	Kartik Shukla Purnima
32.	Sankat Chaturthi	Paus Krishna Pratipada
33.	Makar Sankranti	Magh Krishna Pratipada
34.	Mauni Amavasya	Magh Krishna Amavasya
35.	Vasant Panchami	Magh Shukla Panchami
36.	Mahashivaratri	Phalgun Krishna Chaturthi
37.	Holi	Phalgun Shukla Purnima

1. Christmas
2. New Year
3. Easter
4. Good Friday
5. Ramzan
6. Id-ul-Zuha
7. Id-ul-Fitr
8. Muharram
9. Baravafat
10. Shab-a-Barat
11. Guru Nanak Day
12. Mahavir Jayanti

26th January and 15th August are also celebrated in Uttarakhand with great pomp and show as National Festivals.

FAIRS AND FESTIVALS : AT A GLANCE

1. **Almora:** Shrawan Mela (Jageshwar), Doonagiri Mela (Ranikhet), Gananath Mela, Dwarhat Mela, Kasar Devi Mela, Somnath Fair.

2. **Bageshwar:** Uttarayani Mela, Shivratri Fair, Kartik Purnima, Dussehra Fair.

3. **Champawat:** Purnagiri Fair, Devidhura Fair, Mata Murti Ka Mela.

4. **Dehradun:** Jhanda Fair, Tapakeshwar Fair, Lakshman Siddha Fair, Bissu Fair, Mahasu Devta's Fair, Shadheed Veer Kesari Chand's Fair, Lakhawar Fair, Hanol Mela, Neelkanth Mahadev Mela.

5. **Haridwar:** Ardh Kumbh and Kumbh Mela, Kavand Mela.

6. **Nainital:** Vasantotsav, Nanda Devi Fair, Hariyali Devi Fair, Ranibagh Fair, Chhota Kailash Fair, Garjiadevi Fair, Sharadotsav, Holi Mahotsav.

7. **Pithoragarh:** Jauljibi and Thal Fairs, Punyagiri Mela, Hatkalika Fair.

8. **Tehri Garhwal:** Chandrabadni Fair, Surkhanda Devi Fair, Kunjapuri Fair.

9. **Udham Singh Nagar:** Tharuwat Buxad Mahotsav, Ataria Fair, Chaiti Fair, Terai Utsav.

10. **Uttarkashi:** Magh Mela.

FORESTS

Forests are invaluable treasures provided by nature. These are symbols of our culture, prosperity and progress. These forests check the environment from pollution and enhance the natural beauty and moderate the climate. These forests play an important role in the preservation of the earth and water and give protection to wild animals and make our lives blessed.

Forest of Uttarakhand

Uttarakhand is a rich State in forest resources. The forest area in Uttarakhand is around 24,295 km^2. In this 4,969 km^2 is very dense forests, 12,884 km^2 is moderately dense forests and 6,442 km^2 is open forest. Nearabout 2000 medical herbs are found in the forests of Uttarakhand. There is nearabout yearly income of ₹ 60 crore from the forests of the State.

The forest area of Uttarakhand can be divided into six parts:

(i) Reserved Forest   (ii) Protected Forest

(iii) Unclassified Forest   (iv) State Forest

(v) Communal Forest   (vi) Private Forest

The process for forest preservation started in Uttarakhand in 1800 A.D. At that time, it was banned to cut 'saal forests' in some parts of Dehradun, Kumaon and in marshy regions but from 1855 to 1861, forests were cut on a large scale. As a result, the Commissioner of Kumaon Mr. Ramsay tried his best first time to preserve the 'saal forests'. In 1884, first 'Action Plan for Forest Department' was set up for scientific management of the forests. But during the Second World War, a large number of forests were destroyed. Due to this reason, all the scientific managements for the forests were staggered and it was felt necessary the preservation of the forests from the beginning.

As a result of Zamindari Abolition after independence in 1947, the condition of forests which were included in forest department was deplorable. Therefore, different development programmes were started seeing the necessities of development and preservation of the forests. In 1948, 'Central Forest Council' was set up and Van Mahotsava Programmes were launched on a large scale in 1950. In 1952, National Forest Policy was fixed for the management of different programmes related to forestry. In this series, various forest development programmes for example-afforestation, plantation, improvement in forest information, bordering of forest areas, making list of forest resources and work for making action plans were performed. In spite of this, in 1952, for the protection of wildlife, 'Indian Wildlife Council' was set up seeing the importance for the preservation of wildlife.

Formerly, forests were under the protection of Central Government but in 1935, these forests became the property of the State Government. The organisation of the forest department in the State is generally of the following types :

1. Chief Conservator of forests (Administrator for the forests of the whole State)
2. Conservator of forests (Area Inspector)
3. Deputy (Forest officer)
4. Forest Ranger or Assistant Ranger (Assistant of Deputy Forester)
5. Forest Inspector (one who inspects sub-regions of the forests)
6. Forest guards (the persons who work under foresters)

The forests of the State have been divided in many regions. The inspection of each forest region is done by the conservator of forest. When there are many regions then there is one head, that is conservator of forests who manages the whole forest areas of the State. There are many circles in each forest region. Each circle is divided into various forest areas and sub-areas whose officers are respectively Forester, Deputy Forester, Ranger or Assistant Ranger etc. For the help of foresters, there are Forest guards.

The forest related education is given at 'Indian Forest College' situated at Dehradun city of Uttarakhand. This college was established in 1878 in the name of 'Forest School of Dehradun'. In 1914, a 'Forest Research Institute' was established at Dehradun. Subsequently in 1929, one more Forest research institute was established at Kulagarh (Dehradun). From 1st April, 2001, newly constituted 'Uttarakhand Forest Corporation ' is working independently.

Three types of forests are found in Uttarakhand:

1. Sub-Himadri & Himadri Forests: Such types of forests are found in the regions where heights are between 2900 metres to 3500 metres. Such regions are not suitable for the trees. Thorny small bushes of Junipur, Madhumati creepers *etc.* are found in these forests. Generally, there is a heavy rain in these forest regions but these forest trees are situated on hilly slopes. Due to this reason, water does not stay in the roots of trees.

2. Wet & Equal Sub-tropical Forests of Himalayas: Such types of forests are found in the midst of the chir and Sub-Himadri forest regions from the heights of 1600 to 2900 metres. These forests belong to thorny species and always remain evergreen. The famous trees of these forests are-Deodar, Beech, Birch along with Chinar, Elm, Rododaidron, Chestnut, Maple *etc.* are found.

3. Chir Forest of Sub-Temperate Region: Such types of forests are found in lower Himalayan region between the wet-even tropical forests and damp leafy forest region of Torrid Zone.

Protection of Forests: Due to growth of population and economical reasons, the pressure on the forests is increasing always. As a result, violation of forest rules, theft of forest product, illegal cutting of forests, illegal hunting etc. are increasing day by day. Armed anti-social elements cut the forests illegally and hunt in the forests without permission. The employees of forest department get themselves incapable to check such anti-social elements because they (employees) are unarmed. Therefore, it has become necessary to strengthen the security measures for the protection of the forests. For the inspection and supervision of the forests, 31 Armed Protection group (one head constable and 3 constables per group) and two protection groups, in which 117 ex-soldiers may be appointed.

Industrial & Pulpwood Forestation: Two projects respectively to plant such species of trees which have economic and industrial importance and forestation of such species of trees which have rapid growth. In seventh Five Year Plan, including all above projects, 'Industrial & Pulpwood Forestation Project' was launched. According to this project, wood based industries-match-making, Plywood, hard-board, pertical-board, packing case, catechu, furniture *etc.* and for the supply of necessary items of such industries, adequate species of trees are forestated.

> **MEDICINAL PLANTS**
> - Medicinal plants growing upto 1000 m: bel, chitrak, kachnar, pipali, babul, ashok, amaltas, sarpagandha, bhringraj, harar, behera, malu, siris, amla and mossli.
> - Medicinal plants growing from 1000m to 3000m: banspa, sugandhabala, tejpat, dalchini, jhoola, kuth, timru and painya.
> - Medicinal plants growing above 3000m. atis, mitha, gugal, jamboo, mamira, gandrayan, bajradanti and salammishri.

The running projects in forest department prior to 1991-92 are:

1. Arrangement of trees on both sides of roads **2.** Survey and development of small forest product **3.** Re-emancipation of low category forests. These projects have been-included in 'Industrial Pulpwood Forestation Project.'

Development of Forest-Parks: The importance of forest-parks is increasing day by day due to noisy environment of cities and polluted atmosphere. For this purpose, the forest department has launched this project. According to this project, forest-parks, picnic-spots etc. are being constructed.

Ramganga Water Origin Regional Valley Project: Various soil-preservation programmes such as–land reform, development of pastures, forestation are being done by the forest department at Kalagarh in Ramganga water origin area.

Soil preservation work in the region of Tehri Barrage water origin: Soil preservation and forestation programmes were started in the last phase of 1992-93. Forestation in 18,466 hectares, pasture development and 1,179 small engineering activities were performed.

'Apna Gaon Apna Van' project was started to correlate the villages with forests. According to this project, the trees of Saal, Sagaun, Pine etc. are being planted near the villages.

ANIMALS AND BIRDS

Animals and birds are dependent on trees not only for their food but also for their shelter and habitation. The diversity of animals and birds depends to some extent on the diversity of florae. Different types of animals and birds are found in Uttarakhand. They are of different species. The brief description of these animals and birds which are found here is given as under :

Water animal (Fishes): Fishes like–Mahaser, Hilsa, Saul, Sauli, Tengana, Parina, Rasela, Vittal, Rohu, Mrigal, Katta, Labi, Mangur, Kyuchia, Eel, Singhi, Mirror-carp and trout *etc.* frogs and toads.

Reptiles: Bamania, Pit Viper, Lizard, Iguana, Cobra, Tortoise, Krait, Dhamin, and Crocodile.

| Cobra | Lizard | Crocodile |

Flying Birds: Kite, Vulture, Peacock, Parrot, Cuckoo, Pigeon, Owl, Jay and Sparrow.

Mammals: Bat, Mole, Porcupine, Squirrel, Rabbit, Mongoose, Cow, Buffalo, Goat, Sheep and Pig.

OTHER ANIMALS AND BIRDS

Lion, Panther, Hilly Leopard, Sambhar (Chamois), Cheetal, Kaker, Black deer, Elephant, Neelgay (a white footed antelope), Black-grey bear, Hilly goat, Hilly Sheep, Boa, Hyena, Wild Dog *etc.* Birds like Cock-Peahen, Partridge, Quail, Duck, Nightingale, Goose and Crane and generally found.

Some wild animals of Uttarakhand are becoming extinct. Therefore, hunting of wild animals has been banned.

For the preservation of wild animals, the Government of India passed 'Indian Wildlife (Protection) Act' in 1972. Special arrangement has been made to protect those species of animals about whom there is a danger of extinction. Complete ban has been imposed for the hunting of protected animals and it has been declared punishable crime.

'Indian Wild Animal Board' is famous institute on this subject which advises to the Central Government from time to time. According to 42nd Amendment of the Constitution which was done in 1976, 'Forests and Wild Animals' have been brought under Concurrent List. Accordingly, the State and Central Government can take step for the protection of them. Various animals' Sanctuaries have been established for the protection of rare species of animals in Uttarakhand keeping in view of the protection of wild animals. Considering this point of view, 'Establishment of Nanda Devi Park' and 'Development of Muskdeer Farm' project was accepted in 1990-91. In 1981-82, a project namely 'Compact Management of Animals' Sanctuaries' was accepted. According to this project, the development activities of 'Animals' Sanctuaries of Uttarakhand', 'Kedarnath Animals Sanctuary', 'Valley of Flowers' and National Park Kaimoor *etc.* have been included in this project. In 1991-92, according to this project,' Tiger Watch Project' has also been included in it.

For the preservation of extinct tigers in Uttarakhand, a project namely 'Corbett Park Tigers' Preservation' is being performed with the help of Central Government. According to this project, the preservation, nourishment and breeding of extinct tiger species are studied. In 1983, 'Rajajee National Park' has been established in the area of 820 sq. km including Rajajee, Motipur and Chilla wildlifes sanctuaries of the districts of Dehradun, Saharanpur and Pauri-Garhwal.

In Uttarakhand region, 'Snow-Leopard Project' for the preservation of extinct snow-leopard was formulated. This project came into force in 1990-91.

USES OF DEAD-BODIES OF ANIMALS AND TANNING

A large quantity of leather is produced from the dead bodies of the animals in Uttarakhand. For the good qualities of leather, it is necessary the use of scientific method of tanning for the skins of dead animals. For this purpose, centre for dead bodies' uses has been established at Dehradun.

20 | Rivers and Lakes

FAMOUS RIVERS

Ganga and Yamuna are two famous rivers of Uttarakhand. Its flowing in north is regulated by the Himalayas. The source of Ganga is at Gomukh, where the mighty rivers emerges from the depth of Gangotri glacier. The Gangotri glacier is situated at the height of 5,165 metres above the sea level. Here the river is known as Bhagirathi. Rising in the icy caves of Gangotri glacier, the river Bhagirathi starts its long journey downwards where it joins river Alaknanda and becomes Ganga.

The source of Yamuna river is Yamunotri glacier which is situated at the height of 6,315 metres. This place is very far away from Gangotri. The source of Ghaghra is near Rox Tal. The sources of Sutluj, Sindhu and Brahmaputra rivers are at the long distance of north part of the Himalayan ranges. This river is made up of three streams of the same name. There are another small rivers in the northern part of the plain of Ganga, those are Kosi, Gola, Sai and Kalyani.

The brief description of the famous rivers of Uttarakhand is given below:

The River Ganga: The source of this river is Gomukh glacier which is situated at the height of 5,165 metres above the sea level. Two tributaries of Ganga, Alaknanda and Bhagirathi join it at Devprayag. The river Ganga flows downward near Haridwar following the south and south-west directions. This river flows from Haridwar first in south and after that it flows in south-west direction. At Allahabad, river-Yamuna joins it which is known as Sangam (confluence of rivers). From here, the river flows in the east direction and near Ghazipur joins Gomti and near Ballia joins Ghagra in

Source of Ganga Gomukh Glacier

it. Near Patna joins the Sone river and after some distance the rivers Gandak and Kosi also join the Ganga. After Farakka, the main stream of the river Ganga flowing in east and in south-east enters into Bangladesh and here it is known as Padma. From here, it divides into many streams and flows into sea through Deltaic plain. Many streams Dwarika, Ajay, Roopnarayan, Haldi *etc.* flowing from peninsular plateau join into the river Ganga which is known here in this region as Bhagirathi-Hooghly. In Bangladesh, near Chanderpur before joining the sea, the river Padma joins Brahmaputra which are called there as Yamuna and Meghana. On the banks of this river Ganga, many important cities Haridwar, Rishikesh, Badrinath, Kanpur, Allahabad, Varanasi, Patna, Monghyr, Bhagalpur, Murshidabad *etc.* are situated. The total length of it is 2,510 km.

The River Yamuna: The source of this river is Yamunotri glacier which is situated at the western slope of Banderpoonchh. The river flows in the south-west direction from here. After crossing the Nagatibb mountain range, it joins its tributary the river Tonse. After flowing to some distance of Dehradun district, it crosses the Shivalik range and enters into Uttar Pradesh. It flows in south direction to some distance at this place. This river makes the form of semi-circle. The length of this river is 1,375 km. till it joins the river Ganga at Allahabad. Chambal, Kein, Betwa, Sindhu *etc.* are its tributaries. According to geologists,

*Source of Yamuna
Yamunotri Glacier*

the river Yamuna flowed sometimes in south and south-west directions towards Rajasthan and contemporary Saraswati was its tributary. Delhi, Mathura, Agra, Etawa *etc.* are situated on its banks. The total length of this river is 1,375 km.

Ramganga: The source of this river is somewhat south of main range of the Himalayas in Garhwal district. From its source to 150 km. its movement provides depths and enter into the region of plains. Due to heavy rain in northern part, there is terrible flood in this river. This river joins the Ganga near Kannauj flowing in the south-east direction through Moradabad, Rampur, Bareilly, Badaun and Shahjahanpur–districts along with some

Source of Ramganga at Garwal

parts of Farrukhabad and Hardoi districts. Its total length is 600 km.

River Sharda (Kali): This river flows from Milap glacier eastern Kumaon, and bordering region of Tibet. This river is famous as black river but this river is called Black Ganga in place of black river. This river demarcates the boundary of Kumaon and Nepal. After flowing 160 km, Saryu or East Ganga joins at Pancheshwar, Coming downwards its name changes as Sharda or Gauri Ganga from Black Ganga Yas Kali. Some people call it Saryu also. It enters into the plain near Brahmadev with rippling great speed. This

Source of River Sharda at Kumaon

river demarcates the boundary of Nepal from Pilibhit district. Chaukia river joins this river in Pilibhit. This river joins Ghaghra near Baharamghat flowing with zig-zag snaky movement.

FAMOUS CITIES OF STATE SITUATED ON THE BANKS OF RIVERS

Cities	*Rivers*
Badrinath	Alaknanda
Haridwar	Ganga
Rishikesh	Ganga

LAKES

Lakes are in abundance in Uttarakhand. Most of the lakes are in Kumaon region which are formed due to change in the surface of the earth by the internal forces of the earth. The brief description of the lakes of Uttarakhand is given below:

Bhimtal Lake: This lake is the biggest lake of Kumaon region of Uttarakhand. It is situated at the distance of 10 km north from Kathgodam. It is at the height of 1332 metres from the sea-level. There is an island in the middle of the lake which is made of volcanic rocks. Many canals have been constructed for irrigation purpose from this lake.

Bhimtal Lake

Naukuchiatal Lake: This lake is situated at the distance of 4 km south-east of Bhimtal lake. This lake is at the height of 1292 metres from the sea-level. This lake is 1004 metres long, 750 metre wide and 45 metres deep. It is one of the deepest lake of Kumaon region.

Naini Lake: This lake is also situated in Kumaon region of Uttarakhand in Nainital district. Nainital city is situated on the bank of this lake. Here is the temple of Naini Devi. Possibly, the name of this lake is termed due to this temple. There are high mountains around the lake except the south-east part of it. This lake is 1500 metres long, 510 metres wide and 30 metres deep. Boating is also done in this lake on large scale. Various kinds of fishes are found in this lake.

Naini Lake

Saat Tal Lake: This lake is a group of seven small lakes. It is situated at the distance of 20 km from Nainital. It is 19 metres deep and it is at the height of 1288 metres from sea-level.

Roopkund: This lake is spread in 500 sq. feet area and situated at the height of 4780 metres in Uttarkashi. It is always frozen except the months of August-September. It is also called Kankali-Tal because 600 year old skeletons (Kankals) have been found here.

Deoria-Tal: It is the most attractive lake of Garhwal region near Rudraprayag. Its length is near about 1.5 km and it is full of unique natural scenery.

Sahastra Tal: This lake is situated at the height of near about 5,500 metres in Tehri-Garhwal. It is surrounded by flowers from all sides. In transparent water of this lake below 40 metres, there lie quadrangular benches of stones. It is believed that hermits used to meditate here.

CHIEF CANALS OF THE STATE

The flowing region of the most of canals of Uttarakhand is Uttar Pradesh. The chief canals of Uttarakhand are as given below:

Nanak Sagar Canals: These canals emerge from the dams constructed near Nainital and irrigate near about 1.5 lakh hectare area of Kumaon region.

Ramganga Project Canals: After constructing a dam near Kalagarh of Garhwal district, near about 17.05 lakh acre area of land is being irrigated from near about 3,200 km long canal range.

Sharda Canal: This canal emerges from 'Banbasa' situated at the border of U.P. and Nepal, This canal has length of 12,368 km. Khateema Power House is situated at this canal.

S.No.	Name of Dam	River	Nearest City	Height of the Dam (in metre)
1.	Vyasi	Yamuna	Dehradun	061
2.	Ichari	Tonse	Dehradun	060
3.	Kisau	Tonse	Dehradun	253
4.	Lakhwar	Yamuna	Dehradun	192
5.	Tehri Dam	Bhagirathi	Tehri	261
6.	Maneri Bhali Hydro-Electric Project	Bhagirathi	Uttarkashi	039

FIVE PRAYAGS

1. Vishnuprayag – Alaknanda meets Dhauliganga
2. Nandprayag – Alaknanda meets Mandakini
3. Karnaprayag – Alaknanda meets Pindar
4. Rudraprayag – Alaknanda meets Mandakini
5. Devprayag – Alaknanda meets Bhagirathi

MOUNTAIN RANGES OF UTTARAKHAND

S.No.	Mountain Range	ht from Sea level (mt)	District
1.	Banderpoonch	6,315	Uttarkashi
2.	Nandakot	6,861	Bageshwar
3.	Trishul	7,122	Chamoli
4.	Panchshuli	6,904	Pithoragarh
5.	Dunagiri	7,068	Almora
6.	Kamet	7,756	Chamoli
7.	Mana	7,273	Chamoli
8.	Nanda Devi	7,817	Chamoli
9.	Nanda Devi Purvi	7,434	Chamoli
10.	Chaukhamba	7,183	Chamoli

21 | National Parks and Sanctuaries

Jim Corbett National Park: This national park was established in Nainital in 1936. After Independence Helly National Park is renamed as Ram Ganga National Park. In 1957, it was again renamed as Jim Corbett National Park-(Jim Corbett was famous Wildlife Protector). It is spread in 520.80 square kilometres. This park is an abode of 300 races of wild animals and birds. Lions, tigers *etc.* are found in this park. It is a tiger reserve park.

Nanda Devi National Park: This park lies in Chamoli district at the height of 2400 to 6817 metres and spread in the area of 630 sq. km. It was established in 1980. This park has spectacular natural beauty and famous for rare wild animals.

Valley of Flowers National Park: The famous valley of flowers with the largest concentration of various species of wild flowers is on the Rishikesh–Badrinath road, 16 km from Govindghat. This park was established in 1981. Himalayan black bear, musk-deer and various kinds of birds are found in this park. It is spread in area of 87 sq. km at the height of 3352 to 6500 metres.

Rajajee National Park: This park was founded in 1983 in area of 820 sq. km. Rajaji National Park is distinct for its pristine scenic beauty and rich bio-diversity. Tigers, Bears, elephants, leopards, panthers, chamoises, barking deer, big lizards, boas and various kinds of birds are found in this park. It is a tiger reserve park.

Jim Corbett National Park

Valley of Flowers Natonal Park

Kedarnath Sanctuary: It is situated in Chamoli district in the middle of hills covered with snow and it is spread in the area of 975.20 sq. km. In this area, hilly animals can be seen.

Cheela Wild Life Sanctuary: This sanctuary is situated in area of 249 sq. km. The elephants are found in natural environment between the height of 300 to 1,345 metres, other kinds of animals and birds can also be seen in this sanctuary. This place is situated in Kotdwar region.

Motichoor Sanctuary: This sanctuary is spread in 89 sq. km area of Haridwar district. Rare species of birds and other wild animals are found in this sanctuary.

Askote Sanctuary: This sanctuary is situated in Pithoragarh district and famous for Himalayan tigers, bears, musk-deer, Himalayan birds and natural scenery.

Govind Wild Life Sanctuary: This sanctuary is situated in Uttarkashi district and it is spread in area of 485 sq. km. at the height of 1,300 to 6,315 metres. Tigers, Hyenas, Crocodiles etc. of various species can be seen in this sanctuary.

NATIONAL PARKS OF UTTARAKHAND AT A GLANCE

- Jim Corbett National Park, Ramnagar, Nainital, foundation–1936, area–521 sq. km.
- Nanda Devi National Park, Chamoli, foundation–1980, area–630 sq. km.
- Valley of flowers National Park, Chamoli, foundation–1982, area–87 sq. km.
- Rajaji National Park, Dehradun, Pauri Garhwal & Haridwar-Foundation-1983 area–820 sq. km.
- Gangotri National Park, Uttarkashi, area–2,390 sq. km.
- Govind National Park, Uttarkashi, area–472 sq. km.

WILDLIFE SANCTUARIES OF UTTARAKHAND : AT A GLANCE

S.No.	Name	Foundation year	Area in Square Km	District
1.	Govind Wildlife Sanctuary	1955	485	Uttarkashi
2.	Kedarnath Wildlife Sanctuary	1972	975.20	Chamoli
3.	Askote Wildlife Sanctuary	1986	600	Pithoragarh
4.	Sona Nadi Wildlife Sanctuary	1987	301	Garhwal
5.	Winsor Wildlife Sanctuary	1988	47.07	Almora
6.	Mussourie Wildlife Sanctuary	1993	11	Dehradun
7.	Nandhaur Wildlife Sanctuary	2012	269.96	Nainital & Champawat

22 | Scheduled Castes and Tribes

SCHEDULED CASTES OF THE STATE

1. Agaria	18. Beldar	34. Dharmi	50. Kori
2. Badhik	19. Beriya	35. Dhariya	51. Korwa
3. Badi	20. Bhantu	36. Gond	52. Lalbegi
4. Baheliya	21. Bhuiya	37. Gwal	53. Majhwar
5. Baiga	22. Bhuyiar	38. Habura	54. Mazhabi
6. Baiswar	23. Boria	39. Hari	55. Musahar
7. Bajaniya	24. Chamar, Dhusia, Jhusia, Jatava	40. Hela	56. Nat
8. Bajgi		41. Kalabaz	57. Pankha
9. Balhar	25. Chero	42. Kanjar	58. Parahiya
10. Balai	26. Dabgar	43. Kapariya	59. Pasi, Tarmali
11. Balmiki	27. Dhangar	44. Karwal	60. Patari
12. Bangali	28. Dhanuk	45. Khairaha	61. Sahariya
13. Banmanus	29. Dharkar	46. Kharwar (excluding Banvansi)	62. Sanaurhiya
14. Bansphor	30. Dhobi		63. Sansiya
15. Barwar	31. Dom	47. Khatik	64. Shilpkar
16. Basor	32. Domar	48. Kharot	65. Turaiha
17. Bawariya	33. Dusadh	49. Kol	

The major tribes in Uttarakhand are-Bhotia, Raji, Buksa, Jaunsari, Shauka, Mahigeer and Tharu.

Tharu

They are not only residents of Uttarakhand but they are also found in Uttar Pradesh. They are descendants of Kerats. They originally belong to Thar region of Rajasthan. That is why they are called Tharu. According to some people, the word Thar means wine and Tharu means one who takes wine. They wear dhoti-Kurta and pagri (man) and dark red colour lahenga-choli (woman). Four social divisions are found in this community. Brahmin Buksas are most reputed in them. They are having their social relations with Hindus of the plains. They follow the practice of polygamy, widow remarriage, ghar Jawai pratha. They worship Shiva, Kali, Durga, Rama, Laxmi and Krishna. They grow rice, maize, wheat, gram and laha and their second main occupation is animal rearing.

Houses: The people of Tharu Community are of small stature, broad face and they are generally of yellow colour. The women are beautiful and attractive. The people of Tharu community do not make their houses of bricks and soil. They make their houses of logs of wood and reeds. They make their houses in north-south direction and doors are in east direction. Their houses have many rooms. They also make one room for worship.

Food: Their main food is rice. They also eat fish, milk, curd and meat of hunted animals of the jungles. They also eat eggs and pork. They take their food at right interval and call them with different names. For example–Kalewa (Breakfast), Meejhani (Lunch), Beri (Dinner). They take meat and wine on large scale. Wine is main beverage of Tharus and they drink wine on every occasion. They drink wine made of rice which is called 'Jar'.

Family System: There is united family system. There are many such families of Tharus whose number of members is more than five hundred. Such families are found in the terai of Nepal. The oldestman of the family becomes the head of family. Each member of family works according to his guidance.

Bhotia

This tribe is also called Shauka. They belong to Bhot region of Uttarakhand. They live in northern mountain region near Tibetan-Nepal Border. They belong to Mangol race and their culture is influenced by Tibet. They live in Almora, Pithoragarh, Chamoli and Uttarkashi districts. They follow Hinduism. Ladies of this tribe wear long coat with short sleeves called 'Chung'. They wear a type of Kurta called 'Phuyabel'. They also wear *munge ki mala*. Gents of this tribe wear a long coat with pyjama and pahadi cap.

Religion: The people of Bhotia tribe call themselves Khas or Rajput. All Surnames of Rajputs are found in them. Some of the tribes converted into Buddhism and worship 'Gawala' and 'Bang Ram Chim' gods. They live in high mountainous region. Their summer time home is called 'Mat' and their winter time home is called 'Munsa'. They follow the practice of abduct marriage. Hudka is their famous music instrument. They follow the barter system of business, they bring salt, suhaga, wool, tail of yak, gold, animal skin, sheep and goat etc. in return they give rice, gur, sugar, iron, cotton, tobacco etc. Their main occupation is agriculture and animal rearing.

Jaunsari

The people of Jaunsari Tribe live in high mountains of Uttarakhand at Kalsi, Chakarata, Tyori, Lakhamandal, Jaunsar, Bawar (Dehradun), Jaunpur (Tehri-Garhwal), Raben (Uttarkashi) and Parganekana *etc.* places. They belong to the blood relation of Mangols and doms. They follow the Hindu religion. Jaunsari Tribe is divided in three parts. They are–Khasas, Karigar and Harijan Khasas. In Khasas comes–Brahmins and Rajputs, in Karigar comes blacksmiths, goldsmiths, carpenter, Bajgi and Oad. In Harijan Khasas comes–Dom, Kod, Kolta, Koli and Cobbler *etc.* Men of Jaunsari Tribe wear dhoti-shirt and jacket. Women of Jaunsari tribe wear kurta upto knee and Ghagra. They live in wooden houses of many floors. They practise polyandry and intercaste marriages. Their main occupation is agriculture and workmanship.

Food: The people of Jaunsari tribe drink wine as their favourite beverage. They distil wine at their homes. They eat rice and meat etc.

Festivals: Vissoo (Vaishakhi), Panchoi (Dussehra), Diyai (Deepawali) are their famous festivals. Deepawali is their special festival and this festival is celebrated for one month.

Buksa

The people of Buksa or Bhoksa tribe live in Pauri and Garhwal districts. They live in small village dwellings. Their dense population is found in the Bajpur, Ramnagar and Kashipur regions. They are known to have relation with Patwar Rajpoot. They speak Hindi and their script is Devnagari.

Food: Their principal food is fish and rice. They also eat bread made of maize and wheat, curd and milk *etc.* To eat the meat of monkeys, cows and peacock is restricted in their community.

Dress and Clothes: The people of this tribe wear kurta-dhoti, sadari and turban. Women wear lehnga of dark red colour or blue or black chintz. But at present the women wear saree, blouse, sweater and cardigan. They make their hair lock like the women of Mewati Rajput of Rajasthan. A married woman uses vermilion and wears glass bangles.

Marriage: The system of marriage in Buksa tribe is similar to Hindu system. They follow Anulome and Pratilome System of marriage. Polygamy system is also prevalent. Divorce is got easily in this community. There is a rise in premarital and post-marital sexual relations.

Religion: Buksa tribe worships Mahadeva, Kali, Durga Laxmi, Ram and Krishna. Their religion is similar to Hinduism. Chamunda Devi of Kashipur is considered the most powerful goddess of the tribe. Their festivals are also similar to that of Hindus. Holi, Diwali, Dussehra and Janmashtami are their famous festivals. They worship village goddess outside the village at a place called 'Than'.

Raji

They are also called 'Banraut'. They mainly live in Pithoragarh district. In the pre-historic period at the east of Ganga plateau and upto the Central Nepal was the region belongs to Agnevanshi Kolvirat tribes. They are called by different names such as Raji, Banraut, Banrawat, Banmanush, king of jungles *etc*. But Raji is their popular name. They like to live in jungles and worship forest gods. Their main god is Baghnath. They speak 'Munda 'language at their homes and Kumayuni outside which contains number of Tibetan Sanskrit words. They are very superstitious. They purchase girls and marry them. Women have right to remarriage. Their main business was woodcutting. But after restriction on this occupation, they are working as landless workers. They like to make tattoos on their bodies.

Language: The people of this tribe speak Munda language. For outer communication, they use Kumaoni. As a whole their language is a mixture of Hindi and Pahari.

Festivals: There are two festivals of this tribe. They are–Karka Sankranti and Makara Sankranti. They prepare special dishes on these occasions.

Dress and Clothes: The people of Raji tribe still lie naked. They live in caves and huts.

Occupation: Agriculture is their main profession. They follow Jhumming system of agriculture. They also work as labourers on the roads. They make goods of wood and go to villages to sell them and bring grains from there. The Government is taking steps for their social and political development.

Mahigeer

They live in Kiratpur, Manera, Mandva and Dharanagar. They are basically fisherman and they believe to have relation with Mahabharat period. They speak Khadi Boli. Some of them have converted into Islam. Their main business is fishery but due to restriction on it they are now working as landless labourers.

23

23 | Education System

THE famous universities, institutions and schools of Uttarakhand are given below:

Universities

1. University of Roorkee–Roorkee
2. G.B. Pant Kumaon University–Nainital
3. Gurukul Kangri University–Haridwar
4. G.B. Pant University of Agriculture and Technology–Pantnagar
5. H.N.B. Garhwal University–Srinagar
6. Dev Sanskriti University–Haridwar
7. U.P. Academy of Administration–Nainital
8. Institute of Management Studies–Dehradun

University of Roorkee, Roorkee   Gurukul Kangri University, Haridwar

Research Organisations and Institutes

1. Forest Research Institutes–Dehradun
2. Indian Institute of Petroleum–Dehradun
3. Central Building Research Institute–Roorkee
4. Indian Military Academy–Dehradun

5. Keshav Dev Malviya Institute of Petroleum Exploration–Dehradun

6. Oil and Natural Gas Corporation Ltd.– Dehradun

7. Wadia Institute of Himalayan Geology– Dehradun

8. Wildlife Institute of India–Dehradun

9. Indira Gandhi National Forest Academy– Dehradun

Forest Research Institute

10. Forest Survey of India–Dehradun

11. Indian Institute of Remote Sensing–Dehradun

12. Instrument Research and Development Establishment–Dehradun

13. LBS National Academy of Administration–Mussourie

14. ONGC Women Polytechnic–Dehradun

15. Indian Society of Remote Sensing–Dehradun

16. Directorate of Forest Education–Dehradun

Famous Schools of Uttarakhand

1. The Doon School–Dehradun
2. St. Joseph Academy–Dehradun
3. Woodstock School–Mussourie
4. Welham Girls' High School–Dehradun
5. Doon International School–Dehradun
6. Scholars Home–Dehradun
7. Brightlands School–Dehradun
8. Pine Hall School–Dehradun
9. Carman School–Dehradun

The Doon School

In spite of above-mentioned points, the following facts must be remembered.

- There are 15,297 Primary Schools, 4,948 Junior High Schools, 3,436 High Schools and Intermediate Colleges in the State.

- The State Government is providing facilities for higher education in Information Technology.

- The State Government has made Compulsory the education of computer, sports and N.C.C.

- The State Government has launched a movement 'School Chalo' from Ist July, 2001. In which the boys and the girls of age group from

6-11 years are given text-books free of cost and they are being admitted in Government's schools.

- The State Government has constituted 'Village Education Committee'. In which the Govt. has initiated two plans – 'Shiksha Bandhu' and 'Shiksha Mitra Yojna'.
- The famous 'Roorkee Engineering College' has been assigned 7th I.I.T. institute of the country.
- The ten degree Colleges of Meerut University in Haridwar district have been separated from the Meerut University and affiliated with H.N.B. Garhwal University, Srinagar.
- Thirteen special schools are being opened in the State, in which professional education will be provided to the handicapped.
- The head office of Uttarakhand Secondary Education Board has been established at Ramnagar in Nainital district.

GOVERNMENT POLY-TECHNICS

1. Government Poly-Technics–Kashipur (Udhamsingh Nagar)
2. Government Poly-Technics–Narendranagar (Tehri-Garhwal)
3. Government Poly-Technics–Dwarhat (Almora)
4. Government Poly-Technics–Lohaghat (Champawat)
5. A Government Poly-Technics College started in 1968-1969 at Srinagar Pauri-Garhwal.

LITERACY

- Uttarakhand State has 17th place in literacy in the country.
- The male literacy rate of Uttarakhand is 13th in the country and female literacy rate in Uttarakhand is 20th in the country.
- According to the Census of 2011, the literacy in the State is 78.8%, in which male literacy is 87.4% and female literacy is 70.0%.
- The least literate district of Uttarakhand is Udham Singh Nagar. In which total literacy is 73.10%. The male literacy is 81.10% and female literacy is 64.40%.

Year	Persons	Male	Female
1951	18.93	32.15	4.78
1961	18.05	28.17	7.33
1971	33.26	46.95	18.61
1981	46.06	62.35	25.00
1991	57.75	72.79	41.63
2001	72.28	84.01	60.26
2011	78.80	87.40	70.0

Districtwise Male & Female Literacy Rate

S. No.	District	Literacy Rate		
		Persons 2011	Male 2011	Female 2011
	Uttarakhand	78.80	87.40	70.0
1.	Uttarkashi	75.80	88.80	62.40
2.	Chamoli	82.80	93.40	72.30
3.	Rudra Prayag	83.10	93.90	70.40
4.	Tehri-Garhwal	74.40	89.80	64.30
5.	Dehradun	84.20	89.40	78.50
6.	Pauri-Garhwal	82.0	92.70	72.60
7.	Pithoragarh	82.20	92.70	72.20
8.	Bageshwar	80.0	92.30	69.0
9.	Almora	80.50	92.90	69.90
10.	Champawat	79.80	91.60	68.0
11.	Nainital	83.90	90.10	77.30
12.	Udham Singh Nagar	73.10	81.10	64.40
13.	Haridwar	73.40	81.0	64.80

- The per cent of literacy rate is upto the age of 7 years and above.

24 | Population and Area

Area

Uttarakhand is a frontier State of India. The physical area of this State is 53,483 sq. km. The total physical area of India is 32,87,263 sq.km. and Uttarakhand is 1.6% of it. Uttarakhand has 19th place in the country according to area.

Population

According to the census of 2011, the population of Uttarakhand is 1,00,86,292. The male population was recorded as 51,37,773 and female population is 49,48,519. The total inhabited villages of U.P. nearabout 1 lakh 12 thousand and 803, in which 15,761 villages have come under Uttarakhand State (2001). The total population of Uttarakhand is 0.83% in comparison of total population of the country. This newly formed State is the biggest Himalayan State in population in comparison to other to Himalayan States. Uttarakhand has 21st Place in the country according to population.

The population growth in a decade of the State is 18.81% which is more than 1.11% in comparison of total population growth of the country in a decade which is 17.7%.

Population Density

The density of population is 189 persons per square kilometre which is less than 49.47 per cent in comparison of total population density of the country which is 382 persons per square kilometre. The highest density of population lies in Haridwar district (801) and the lowest population density lies in Uttarkashi district (41).

The biggest and the smallest districts on the basis of population

The biggest district of the State is Haridwar (18,90,422) and smallest district is Rudra Prayag (2,42,285) on the basis of population.

Literacy

The total number of literate persons in Uttarakhand is 68,80,953. The number of male literates is 38,63,708 and number of female literates is 30,17,245. The percentage of literacy in the State is 78.8% in which male literacy is 87.4% and female literacy is 70.00 per cent. Uttarakhand has 13th place in male literacy and 20th place in female literacy in the country.

Sex Ratio

The sex ratio of Uttarakhand is 963 according to the census of 2011. It means that the number of females on 1000 males is 963. According to last census (2001), it was 962. It shows that the number of female has increased by 1 during the past decade.

SERIAL OF DISTRICTS ON THE BASIS OF POPULATION—2011

Code	District	Population 2011
1.	Haridwar	1890422
2.	Dehradun	1696694
3.	Udham Singh Nagar	1648902
4.	Nainital	954605
5.	Pauri-Garhwal	687271
6.	Almora	622506
7.	Tehri-Garhwal	618931
8.	Pithoragarh	483439
9.	Chamoli	391605
10.	Uttarkashi	330086
11.	Bageshwar	259898
12.	Champawat	259648
13.	Rudra Prayag	242285

Serial of Districts according to Sex-Ratio

Code	State/District	Sex Ratio (No. of females on 1000 males)
	Uttarakhand	**963**
1.	Almora	1139
2.	Rudra Prayag	1114
3.	Pauri-Garhwal	1103

Code	State/District	Sex Ratio (No. of females on 1000 males)
4.	Bageshwar	1090
5.	Tehri-Garhwal	1077
6.	Pithoragarh	1020
7.	Chamoli	1019
8.	Champawat	980
9.	Uttarkashi	958
10.	Nainital	934
11.	Udham Singh Nagar	920
12.	Dehradun	902
13.	Haridwar	880

Districtwise Distribution of Population

S. No.	State-District	Population 2011		
		Persons	Male	Female
1	2	3	4	5
	Uttarakhand	10086292	5137773	4948519
1.	Uttarkashi	330086	168597	161489
2.	Chamoli	391605	193991	197614
3.	Rudra Prayag	242285	114589	127696
4.	Tehri-Garhwal	618931	297986	320945
5.	Dehradun	1696694	892199	804495
6.	Pauri-Garhwal	687271	326829	360442
7.	Pithoragarh	483439	239306	244133
8.	Bageshwar	259898	124326	135572
9.	Almora	622506	291081	331425
10.	Champawat	259648	131125	128523
11.	Nainital	954605	493666	460939
12.	Udham Singh Nagar	1648902	858783	790119
13.	Haridwar	1890422	1005295	885127

Change in Population in a Decade from 1951
Districtwise (in per cent)

S. No.	State-District	Per cent of Change in a decade					
		1951-61	1961-71	1971-81	1981-91	1991-2001	2001-11
1	2	3	4	5	6	7	8
	UTTARAKHAND	22.57	24.42	27.45	24.23	19.20	18.81
1.	Uttarkashi	15.82	20.33	29.19	25.54	22.72	11.89
2.	Udham Singh Ngr.	74.93	41.30	48.16	44.35	27.79	33.45
3.	Almora	13.67	15.14	15.80	9.43	3.14	–1.64
4.	Chamoli	18.89	17.58	24.83	21.97	13.51	5.74
5.	Champawat	27.73	51.39	25.34	26.38	17.56	15.63
6.	Tehri-Garhwal	13.10	14.20	24.67	16.59	16.15	2.35
7.	Dehradun	18.61	34.57	31.93	34.66	24.71	32.33
8.	Nainital	69.54	32.14	38.26	29.87	32.88	25.13
9.	Pauri-Garhwal	14.15	14.56	15.27	9.05	3.87	–1.41
10.	Pithoragarh	19.96	12.98	16.38	14.11	10.92	4.58
11.	Bageshwar	14.19	24.17	18.98	15.50	9.21	5.15
12.	Rudra Prayag	13.31	12.71	24.68	17.40	13.44	6.53
13.	Haridwar	18.01	32.93	32.72	28.44	26.30	30.63

Sex Ratio from the year 1951 (Districtwise)

S.No.	State/District	Sex Ratio (No. of females on 1000 males)						
		1951	1961	1971	1981	1991	2001	2011
1	2	3	4	5	6	7	8	9
	Uttarakhand	940	947	940	936	936	962	963
1.	Uttarkashi	993	964	899	881	918	941	958
2.	Udham Singh Ngr.	731	726	774	841	863	902	920
3.	Almora	1060	1114	1100	1095	1099	1147	1139
4.	Chamoli	1092	1103	1035	1020	982	1017	1019
5.	Champawat	956	929	955	947	945	1024	980
6.	Tehri-Garhwal	1122	1196	1179	1081	1048	1051	1077
7.	Dehradun	715	766	770	811	843	893	902
8.	Nainital	699	715	837	847	881	906	934
9.	Pauri-Garhwal	1137	1163	1119	1091	1058	1104	1103

S.No.	State/District	Sex Ratio (No. of females on 1000 males)						
		1951	1961	1971	1981	1991	2001	2011
1	2	3	4	5	6	7	8	9
10.	Pithoragarh	1020	1052	1033	1027	992	1031	1020
11.	Bageshwar	1008	1024	1057	1031	1055	1110	1090
12.	Rudra Prayag	1144	1169	1169	1121	1094	1117	1114
13.	Haridwar	806	796	803	817	846	868	880

Religious Population of Uttarakhand-2011

	Religious Followers	Percentage of Religious Population	Sex Ratio	Percentage decadal change (2001-11)
1.	Hindus	83.0	976	16
2.	Muslims	13.9	901	39
3.	Sikhs	2.3	912	11.5
4.	Christians	0.4	944	39.3
5.	Buddhists	0.1	675	20
6.	Jains	0.1	934	0.7

DISTRICTWISE POPULATION DENSITY—2011

Code	District	Density
1.	Haridwar	801
2.	Udham Singh Nagar	649
3.	Dehradun	549
4.	Nainital	225
5.	Almora	198
6.	Tehri-Garhwal	170
7.	Champawat	147
8.	Pauri-Garhwal	129
9.	Rudra Prayag	122
10.	Bageshwar	116
11.	Pithoragarh	068
12.	Chamoli	049
13.	Uttarkashi	041

25 Art and Culture

Uttarakhand is a rich State in Art and Culture. Its folk music and folkdances show the importance of hilly culture. The description of its folk music and folk dances are given as under:

FOLK MUSIC

There is a glance of folk customs and cultures in Kumaoni and Garhwali folk songs.

FOLK DANCE

Chaufula Dance: It is a folkdance of Garhwal-full of aesthetic feelings. It is like Gujarati Garba and Garbi.

Jagar: This dance is performed to invite gods and goddesses. It is supposed that invited god comes on the dancer. This dance is also performed to invite god to punish a sinner.

Chaufula Dance

Thadia: This dance is performed during the period of Basant Panchami to Sankranti by ladies.

Jhoda/Chachari: The youths of Kumaoni region perform this dance during moonlight.

Jhumailo: This dance is performed by unmarried girls of Garhwal. It is expressed in forms of tunes.

IMPORTANT DIALECTS OF UTTARAKHAND

Kumaoni: This dialect is spoken in Kumaon region of the State.

Tehiryali: This dialect is spoken in Tehri-Garhwal region of the State.

Garhwali Women   Kumaoni people   Kumaoni women   Bhotia Girl

Jaunsari: This dialect is spoken by Jaunsar-Babar of Dehradun and at high altitudes of Garhwal region.

Bhotia: This dialect is spoken in border areas of Uttarakhand connected with Tibet and Nepal.

Garhwali: It is spoken in Garhwal region of Uttarakhand.

PAINTING

Many artists and painters have gained name and fame throughout the world by their arts and paintings. There is an arrangement for the study of arts and painting in Kumaon and Garhwal Universities for the progress of arts in the State.

Garhwal Painting

❖ — ❖ — ❖

26 | Transportation

FOR the manifold development of the State, the cooperation of transport is very important. The topography of Uttarakhand is varying from place to place. Uttarakhand is having mountains, river valleys and plains also. The total tarcoal (pucka) road length in Uttarakhand is 43,762 km (2016-17). Haldwani, Kathgodam, Haridwar, Kashipur, Lalkuan, Rishikesh, Ramnagar, Roorkee and Dehradun are connected with Railways. Ganga, Yamuna Bhagirathi, Kali, Dholiganga, Ramganga and Tonse rivers are used for small-scale navigation also.

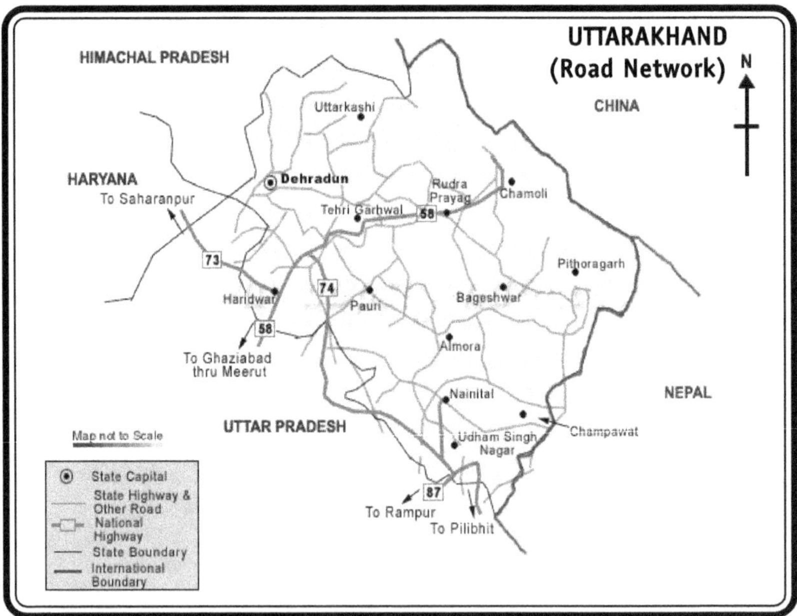

ROAD TRANSPORT

For the transport in Uttarakhand, nearabout 34 thousand kilometres long roads have been constructed. The State highways are connected with both metalled and unmetalled roads. The bus service is main source of transport in Uttarakhand. The bus services are available for Uttarakhand from U.P., Haryana, Delhi, Rajasthan and Himachal Pradesh *etc.*

Uttarakhand's total length of road network was 43,762 km. According to the National Highway Authority of India (NHAI), the National Highways running through the state had a total length of 2954 km in 2016-17.

Till March 2017 road length under PWD was 33,088 km.

RAIL TRANSPORT

Due to hilly region, the rail transport in Uttarakhand is not satisfactory. Haridwar, Dehradun, Kathgodam, Haldwani, Roorkee, Kotdwar, Kashipur and

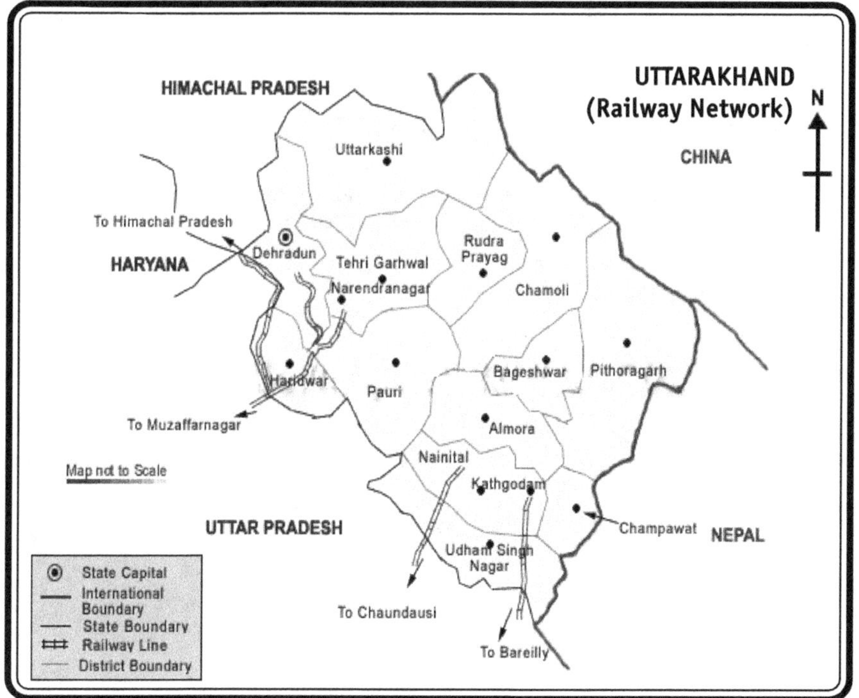

Lalkuan *etc.* are railway stations of Uttarakhand. On 3rd March, 2001, Government has also started a new rail line between Kathgodam and Dehradun.

Some other important trains of Uttarakhand are: Shatabdi Express (Dehradun to New Delhi), Dehradun-Delhi Express (Dehradun to Delhi), Mussourie Express (Dehradun to Delhi), Dehradun Express (Dehradun to Howrah).

Uttarakhand had 345 km of rail routes in 2015-16. The state is focussing on increasing the share of railways in cargo and passenger transport. Initiatives have been made to start monorails at Dehradun, Haridwar and Rishikesh, on the inter-city linkage routes.

AIR TRANSPORT

At present the following aerodromes are there in Uttarakhand State. They are Pant Nagar (Udham Singh Nagar), Naini-Saini (Pithoragarh) Jolly Grant (Dehradun), One Swedish Organisation "Swiss Connect" is also building a small aerodrome at Bajpur. Kumaon and Garhwal Region Development Corporation is also planning for innovative scheme by which tourist can visit distant places with the help of Helicopters. Runways are being constructed at Gauchar (Chamoli) and Chinyalisaur (Uttarkashi).

- All flights connect the state to Delhi.
- Upgradation work is underway at the Jolly Grant airport to facilitate international flights.
- Because of the hilly terrain, the Government has allocated US$ 230,000 for the construction of at least, one helipad per district.
- The state intends to position air-transport as a reliable all-weather transport option for the hills.

WATER TRANSPORT

There is arrangement for navigation in Ganga, Yamuna and other rivers of the State, Small and big boats are used for transport to visit nearby places.

27 First in The State

- The **First Governor** of Uttarakhand was Mr. Surjeet Singh Barnala.
- The **First Chief Minister** of Uttarakhand was Mr. Nityanand Swami.
- The **First Chief Justice** of Uttarakhand High Court was Justice Ashok A. Desai.
- The **First Engineering College** of Uttarakhand was established in 1847 at Roorkee.
- The **First Public School** was established by Mr. C. Das in 1935. This school is presently called Doon Public School.
- The **Biggest District in Area** of Uttarakhand is Chamoli.
- The **Smallest District in Area** of Uttarakhand is Champawat.
- The **Biggest District in Population** of Uttarakhand is Haridwar.
- The **Smallest District of Uttarakhand in Population** is Rudra Prayag.
- The **Highest Peak** of Uttarakhand is Nanda Devi and its height is 7817 metres.
- The **First National Park** of not only the State but of India was founded in 1936 in the name of Helly Park which was renamed after Independence as Ram Ganga Park. Now, this park is called Jim Corbett National Park.
- The **Longest River** of the State is Ganga.
- The **Biggest Lake** of the State is Bhimtal Lake.
- The **Most Literate District** of Uttarakhand is Dehradun.
- The **Least Literate District** of the State is Udham Singh Nagar.
- Mussourie is such place where **Rainfall is the Highest**.

28 | Miscellaneous

UTTARAKHAND STATE PUBLIC SERVICE COMMISSION

The State Public Service Commission has been constituted. It has a Chairman and four members. N.P. Nawani had been appointed as the first Chairman of the State Public Service Commission. The Commission has the right to select Basic, Secondary and Senior Secondary Schools employees and teachers. The head office of the Commission is at Haridwar.

LAW AND ORDER IN UTTARAKHAND

The officials and police of U.P. serving more than one year in Uttarakhand have been accepted as the employees of Uttarakhand. The Police Stations, District Police Headquarters and other important places have been connected with 'State Control Room'. 'Special Task Force' has been constituted to meet the challenges of forest and wine dons. The Central Government has given 11 crore rupees for modernisation and to make the police department lively.

UTTARAKHAND PLANNING COMMISSION

The State Government constituted 'Planning Commission' for the State on 21st March, 2001. Senior M.L.A. Mr. Bharat Singh Rawat had been appointed first Deputy Chairman of the Commission. Planning Directorate and Secretariat have been constituted.

ABOLITION OF CHILD LABOUR

Child labour is one of the major problems of Uttarakhand. The life of this region is full of struggles due to its uneven land, unequal physical features and unemployment. The reason of child labour is poverty, illiteracy and non-implementation of Poverty Abolition Programme. Child labour is seen everywhere whether it may be small towns, blocks or districts. The newly formed Government is trying its hard to remove this blot of child labour.

UTTARAKHAND : SPORTS

A State level stadium is being established at Tehri and New Tehri. To develop the sports in the State, the sportsmen of international fame like Manser Singh, Abhinav Bindra, Jaspal Rana are being consulted and asked for cooperation. 'Sports Academy' at Dehradun is being founded.

SOCIETY, WOMEN WELFARE AND CHILD DEVELOPMENT

The State Government of Uttarakhand is trying its best for the prosperity of the weaker section of society. Many programmes have launched for the betterment of the people. A training centre is being run at Roorkee (Haridwar) for the training of Scheduled Castes and Scheduled tribes candidates for their pre-engineering test for admission. One State workshop has been-established in the district of Nainital, Tehri-Garhwal and Pithoragarh for the training of physically handicapped. For old and weak women, a residential home is being managed at Chamoli having the capacity of 50 inmates.

For the rehabilitation of prostitutes, 'Nari Niketans 'have been established each having capacity of 50 at Tehri-Garhwal, Uttarkashi and Dehradun.

According to Immoral Traffic Preventive Act, District Shelters have been established at Dehradun, Haldwani, Kotdwar and Tehri-Garhwal where morally jeopardised women are kept as per order of the court. They are provided food, clothes and residence free of cost there.

'Shishu Sadan' has been established at Almora for abandoned and orphan babies.

For orphan girls, a school namely 'Ashram Paddhati Vidyalaya' has been established at Bageshwar. Its capacity is for 100 girls. The girls reading in this school get boarding and lodging facilities free of cost.

NAMES OF RESIDENTIAL UNITS

Uttarakhand

1. Log Cabin, Nainapeak, Nainital
2. Paryatak Lodge-Kathgodam, Nainital
3. Paryatak Awas Grih-Kashipur-Udham Singh Nagar
4. Swagat Kendra-Mallital, Nainital
5. Paryatak Awas Grih-Bhimtal, Nainital

6. Paryatak Awas Grih–Sat-tal, Nainital
7. Paryatak Awas Grih–Tallital, Nainital
8. Paryatak Awas Grih–Ram Nagar, Nainital
9. Paryatak Awas Grih–Ranikhet, Almora
10. Holy Day Home–Almora
11. Paryatak Awas Grih–Kausani, Almora
12. Paryatak Awas Grih–Loharkhet, Almora
13. Paryatak Awas Grih–Dhakuri, Almora
14. Paryatak Awas Grih–Khati, Almora
15. Paryatak Awas Grih–Furikaya, Almora
16. Paryatak Awas Grih–Pithoragarh
17. Paryatak Awas Grih–Lohaghat, Pithoragarh
18. Paryatak Awas Grih–Chaukori, Pithoragarh
19. Paryatak Awas Grih–Champawat, Pithoragarh
20. Paryatak Awas Grih–Dwali, Almora
21. Paryatak Awas Grih–Jogeshwar, Almora
22. Paryatak Awas Grih–Bageshwar, Bageshwar
23. Paryatak Awas Grih–Janakpur, Nainital
24. Paryatak Awas Grih–Nanakmatta, Nainital
25. Paryatak Awas Grih–Mawali, Nainital
26. Tourist Dormitory (on the way of Kailash Mansarovar Pilgrimage) Pithoragarh
27. Tourist Dormitory, Jipti (on the way of Kailash Mansarovar Pilgrimage)
28. Tourist Dormitory Goonji (on the way of Kailash Mansarovar Pilgrimage)
29. Paryatak Awas Grih Binso, Almora
30. Paryatak Awas Grih Sheetalakhet, Almora
31. Paryatak Awas Grih Poornagiri, Pithoragarh
32. Tourist Dormitory, Kalapani (on the way of Kailash Mansarovar Pilgrimage), Pithoragarh
33. Tourist Dormitory, Budi (on the way of Kailash Mansarovar Pilgrimage), Pithoragarh
34. Dormitory Sukhatal–Nainital
35. Paryatak Awas Grih, Ramnagar Extension, Nainital
36. Paryatak Awas Grih–Tallital, Nainital
37. Paryatak Awas Grih–Mukteshwar, Nainital
38. Paryatak Awas Grih–Tanakpur, II phase, Nainital
39. Paryatak Awas Grih–Chilithanaula, Almora
40. Paryatak Awas Grih–Deedeehat, Pithoragarh
41. Paryatak Awas Grih–Baijnath, Almora
42. Paryatak Awas Grih–Pangoo, Pithoragarh
43. Paryatak Awas Grih–Haridwar
44. Adhunik Swagat Kendra, Haridwar

GARHWAL REGION

1. Paryatak Awas Grih, Srinagar (New)
2. Paryatak Awas Grih, Srinagar (old)
3. Paryatak Awas Grih, Kotdwar, Pauri
4. Paryatak Awas Grih, Devprayag, Tehri
5. Paryatak Awas Grih, Cheela, Pauri
6. Paryatak Awas Grih, Jwalpadham, Pauri
7. Paryatak Awas Grih, Pauri
8. Paryatak Awas Grih, Kanwashram, Pauri
9. Paryatak Lodge, Gaurikund, Chamoli
10. Paryatak Lodge, Kedarnath, Chamoli
11. Hotel Himlok, Kedarnath, Chamoli
12. Yatri Lodge, Badrinath, Chamoli
13. Paryatak Awas Grih–Ghangharia, Chamoli

14. Hotel Himlok, Badrinath, Chamoli
15. Paryatak Vishram Grih–Nandprayag, Chamoli
16. Yatri Lodge, Karnaprayag, Chamoli
17. Paryatak Awas Grih–Gwaldam, Chamoli
18. Paryatak Awas Grih-Rudra Prayag, Chamoli
19. Paryatak Awas Grih-Guptkashi, Chamoli
20. Paryatak Awas Grih-Mundoli, Chamoli
21. Paryatak Awas Grih-Van, Chamoli
22. Paryatak Awas Grih-Peepalkothi, Chamoli
23. Yatri Chhadak-Muni-Ki-Reti, Tehri
24. Paryatak Vishram Grih-Chandranagar, Chamoli
25. Paryatak Awas Grih-Uttarkashi
26. Yatri Lodge-Uttarkashi
27. Yatri Chhadak-Lanka, Uttarkashi
28. Paryatak Awas Grih-Gangotri, Uttarkashi
29. Yatri Lodge, Bhairavghati, Uttarkashi
30. Yatri Lodge-Sayanachati, Uttarkashi
31. Yatri Lodge, Barkote, Uttarkashi
32. Yatri Lodge, Janakichatti, Uttarkashi
33. Paryatak Awas Grih-Chamba, Tehri
34. Paryatak Awas Grih-Dhanolti, Tehri
35. Paryatak Awas Grih-Arakote, Uttarkashi
36. Paryatak Awas Grih-Bhojwasa, Uttarkashi
37. Paryatak Awas Grih-Hanumanchatti, Uttarkashi
38. Paryatak Awas Grih-Sahastradhara, Dehradun
39. Paryatak Awas Grih-Dak Pathar, Dehradun
40. Hotel Drona, Dehradun
41. Paryatak Awas Grih, Mussourie, Dehradun
42. Paryatak Awas Grih-Gochar, Chamoli
43. Paryatak Awas Grih-Lansdowne, Pauri
44. Paryatak Awas Grih-Chopta, Chamoli
45. F.R.P. Huts, Kedarnath, Chamoli
46. Paryatak Awas Grih-Ukhimath, Chamoli
47. Paryatak Awas Grih-Dewal, Chamoli
48. F.R.P. Huts-Sonprayag, Chamoli
49. Paryatak Awas Grih-Auli, Chamoli
50. Fibre Awas Grih-Auli, Chamoli
51. Paryatak Awas Grih-Dhuttu, Tehri
52. Paryatak Awas Grih (Deluxe)-Rudra Prayag, Chamoli
53. Paryatak Awas Grih-Gopeshwar, Chamoli
54. Paryatak Awas Grih-Chandra Badani, Tehri
55. Paryatak Awas Grih-Purola, Uttarkashi
56. Paryatak Awas Grih-Rixun, Pauri
57. Paryatak Awas Grih-Rambara, Chamoli
58. Paryatak Awas Grih-Srinagar (Srikote), Pauri
59. Paryatak Awas Grih-Harsil, Uttarkashi
60. Paryatak Awas Grih-Joshimath (Chamoli)
61. Paryatak Awas Grih-Gangi, Tehri Garhwal
62. Paryatak Awas Grih-Roh, Tehri
63. Paryatak Awas Grih-Saund, Uttarkashi
64. Paryatak Awas Grih-Osala, Uttarkashi
65. Paryatak Awas Grih-Taluka, Uttarkashi

29 Personalities

POLITICIANS

✦ **Pt. Govind Vallabh Pant:** He was one of the great leaders of Congress. His cooperation in freedom fighting was unique. After Independence, he was awarded Bharat Ratna. He was the first Chief Minister of U.P.

✦ **Badri Prasad Pandey:** He was an important personality in Haldwani Summit and rose the voice for special status for mountainous area in 1946. He was also known as 'Kumaon Kesari'. He has also written a book named 'Kumaon Ka Itihas'.

Pt. Govind Vallabh Pant

✦ **Hemawati Nandan Bahuguna:** Famous freedom fighter, after Independence held many portfolios in Central Government. He was also the Chief Minister of U.P.

LITTERATEUR

✦ **Sumitra Nandan Pant:** He was the famous Hindi poet of Chhayawad (related to nature) and he was related to Kausani. He was the recipient of Bharatiya Jnanpith Award.

✦ **Gumani Pant:** He played an important role for the development of Hindi and local Pahari language.

✦ **Shailesh Matiyani:** He was a famous writer of Almora. He wrote on Social relation. He wrote near about 24 novels and 15 collection of stories. He got Sharda Samman, Lohia Samman and Sadhana Samman. He died on 24th April, 2001.

Sumitra Nandan Pant

✦ **Dr. Hemchandra Joshi:** He was an Editor of famous Hindi Magazine 'Dharmayug'.

Chandra Singh Garwali

✦ **Dev Singh Danoo:** He was very close associate of Netajee Subhash Chandra Bose. He worked on many post in the army formed by Netajee.

✦ **Chandra Singh Garwali:** He was the leader of 'Peshawar Kand' and played an important role in 1930 Freedom Struggle Movement.

✦ **Sarla Ben:** She was a British National. Her original name was Hylamen. She was very much influenced by Gandhiji and he named her Sarla.

_______________ **ARMY OFFICIALS** _______________

Gen. B.C. Joshi

✦ **General B.C. Joshi:** He was born in Almora and he was posted as the Chief of Army Staff and died on duty.

OTHER GREAT PERSONALITIES

_______________ **POLITICIANS** _______________

✦ **Mr. Nityanand Swami:** He was the first C.M. of newly formed State Uttarakhand. He remained the Chief Minister of State from 9th November 2000 to 29th October 2001. Before it, he was the Chairman of U.P. State Legislative Council.

✦ **Mr. Bhagat Singh Koshiyari:** Mr. Koshiyari was the minister in Nityanand Swami Government and has honour to be the 2nd Chief Minister of Uttarakhand. He is regarded as a good organiser.

✦ **Dr. Murli Manohar Joshi:** He was the Professor of Physics in Allahabad University. He is a senior leader of BJP.

Dr. Murli Manohar Joshi

✦ **Mr. Narayan Dutta Tiwari:** He is the senior leader of Congress. He participated in freedom struggle whole heartedly. He had been the C.M. of Uttar Pradesh three times. He has honour to be the Chief Minister of Uttarakhand also.

✦ **Mr. K.C. Pant:** Freedom fighter, senior leader of Congress, Ex-Deputy Chairman of Planning Commission.

✦ **Mr. Satpal Maharaj:** He is a famous spiritual guru who has also participated in politics.

+ **B.C. Khanduri:** He is a senior leader of BJP. He has honour to be the 4th Chief Minister of Uttarakhand.

+ **Dr. Indira Hridayesh:** She is a famous educationist and senior leader of Uttarakhand Congress. She was a cabinet minister in Harish Rawat ministry.

+ **Mr. Pooran Chandra Sharma:** He is a senior leader of Uttarakhand Bhartiya Janata Party.

B.C. Khanduri

+ **Vijay Bahuguna:** He is senior leader of BJP. From March 13, 2012 to January 31, 2014 he was Chief Minister of Uttarakhand.

+ **Mr. Harish Rawat:** He is a senior leader of Congress. He has honour to be the 8th Chief Minister of Uttarakhand.

+ **Dr. Islam Ahmed Siddiqui:** He was born in 'Van Bhool Pura' of Haldwani and was initially Deputy Assistant Secretary in Agriculture Department of America and later on selected for Deputy Minister in the Clinton Government.

Harish Rawat

+ **Dr. Ramesh Pokhariyal 'Nishank':** He is a young leader of BJP. He was the 5th Chief Minister of Uttarakhand.

LITTERATEURS

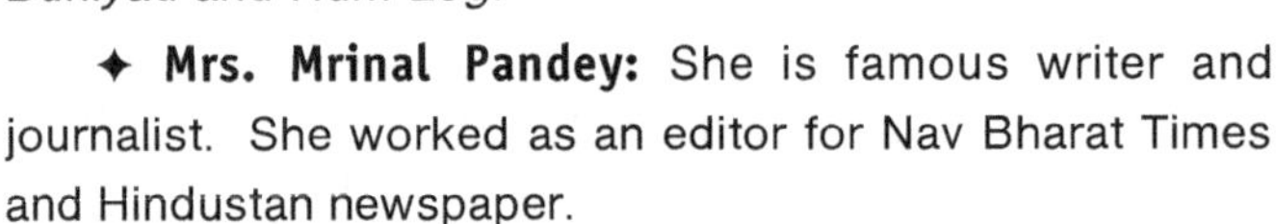

+ **Smt. Gaura Pant 'Shivani':** She has been rewarded many times for her Hindi write-ups of stories and novels. She died in year 2003.

+ **Mr. Himanshu Joshi:** Famous Hindi writer of novels and stories. His many writings have become famous.

+ **Mr. Manohar Shyam Joshi:** He was a famous writer, editor and journalist. He had also presented famous serial *Buniyad* and *Hum Log*.

Mr. Manohar Shyam Joshi

+ **Mrs. Mrinal Pandey:** She is famous writer and journalist. She worked as an editor for Nav Bharat Times and Hindustan newspaper.

+ **Mr. Pawan Tiwari:** He is a young journalist. He gave a new direction to Uttarakhand Movement by his writing. He has edited many magazines successfully.

✦ **Mrs. Urmila Rani Suri:** She has won the National Teacher Prize of Year 2000.

✦ **Mr. M.D. Upadhyay:** He is a famous educationist. He had been the Vice Chancellor of Kumaon University.

✦ **Dr. Shiv Prasad Dabaral:** He is a famous writer and earned familiarity in the field of serious thinking.

✦ **Dr. Pushpesh Pant:** He is famous as writer and thinker in Delhi.

ENVIRONMENTALISTS

✦ **Mr. Chandi Prasad Bhatt:** He is famous environmental scientist who was honoured by Raman Magsaysay Award. He belongs to Chamoli.

✦ **Mr. Sunderlal Bahuguna:** He is the founder father of 'Chipko Movement'. He is a famous environmentalist and honoured with many awards.

SPORTSMEN

✦ **Ms. Bachhendri Pal:** She is the first Indian lady who has privilege of mountaineering Everest successfully in the year 1984. There after she also climbed Mount Black (1986) Kailash (1989), Kamet and Gameen. She has received 'Arjun Puraskar', 'Padmashree', 'National Adventure Puraskar', I.M.F. Gold Medal and a lot more.

Ms. Bechhendri Pal

✦ **Mr. Jaspal Rana:** He is a famous shooter and has received a number of medals in different tournaments in India and abroad. Govt. of India has also honoured him with 'Arjun Puraskar' for the year 1994. He has also received a number of medals in Commonwealth Games held at Kualalampur.

BUREAUCRATS

✦ **Mr. Kamal Pandey:** He was a high official of Indian Administrative Service. He has worked as a Home Secretary in Central Government.

✦ **Mr. Vinod Pandey:** He was a senior officer of Indian Administrative Service. He has also worked as Cabinet Secretary in Central Government.

✦ **Mr. B. D. Pandey:** An I.A.S. officer. He has served as Cabinet Secretary in Central Government.

❖—❖—❖

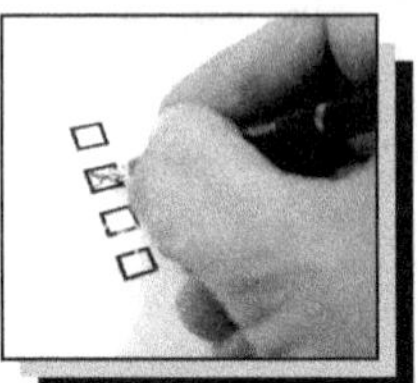

Multiple Choice Questions

1. Separate Uttarakhand came into existence on–
   A. 9th Nov. 2000
   B. 1st Nov 2000
   C. 5th Nov. 2000
   D. 7th Nov. 2000

2. The borders of the countries which touch Uttarakhand State–
   A. Tibet-Bangladesh
   B. Tibet-Nepal
   C. Nepal-Pakistan
   D. Tibet-Pakistan

3. The serial of Uttarakhand in newly formed States on November, 2000 is–
   A. 25th
   B. 26th
   C. 27th
   D. 28th

4. The highest peak of Uttarakhand is-
   A. Trishul
   B. Nandadevi
   C. Panchachuli
   D. Nandakote

5. The first politician who supported for separate Uttarakhand State was–
   A. Pt. Govind Vallabh Pant
   B. Pt. Jawahar Lal Nehru
   C. Smt. Indira Gandhi
   D. Rajeev Gandhi

6. The number of districts in Uttarakhand is–
   A. 13
   B. 14
   C. 15
   D. 16

7. The first Commission constituted for Uttarakhand was–
   A. Pant Commission
   B. Fazal Ali Commission
   C. Kaushik Commission
   D. None of these

8. By which name is Shivalik range of Uttarakhand near Haridwar known as–
   A. Churia
   B. Dundawa
   C. Rishikesh
   D. Nahan

9. For which natural resource is Uttarakhand thought to be rich–
   A. Forest resource
   B. Mineral resource
   C. Gas resource
   D. Water resource

10. Which hilly place is situated on the highest altitude in Uttarakhand?
    A. Mussourie
    B. Dehradun
    C. Nainital
    D. Ranikhet

11. The first local leader who thought for the constitution of separate Uttarakhand State was–
    A. Pt. Govind Vallabh Pant   B. Badri Dutta Pandey
    C. Narayan Dutta Tiwari   D. Dr. Murli Manohar Joshi

12. Which place is the source of upper Ganga canal in Uttarakhand?
    A. Banbasa   B. Okhla   C. Narora   D. Haridwar

13. The first political party formed for the constitution of separate Uttarakhand State is–
    A. BJP   B. Uttarakhand Kranti Dal
    C. Indian National Congress   D. Samajvadi Party

14. On which river's bank is Rishikesh situated in Uttarakhand?
    A. Ganga   B. Yamuna   C. Ghaghra   D. Sharda

15. The first All Parties Conference was organised for separate Uttarakhand at–
    A. Pauri-Garhwal   B. Nainital   C. Karnaprayag   D. Dehradun

16. The area of Uttarakhand is–
    A. 59,950 sq. km   B. 53,960 sq. km
    C. 57,970 sq. km   D. 53,483 sq. km

17. Where is Sat-tal Lake in Uttarakhand?
    A. Nainital   B. Almora   C. Garhwal   D. Dehradun

18. The first procession for separate Uttarakhand in New Delhi was organised in–
    A. 1985   B. 1986   C. 1987   D. 1989

19. In which districts of Uttarakhand is rock phosphate being excavated by Pyrites Phosphates & Chemical Limited?
    A. Garhwal-Nainital   B. Dehradun-Tehri Garhwal
    C. Dehradun-Udham Singh Nagar   D. Champawat-Pithoragarh

20. The first U.P. Government which sent proposal for separate Uttarakhand to Central Government is–
    A. Samajvadi Party Government   B. Congress Government
    C. BSP Govt.   D. BJP Government

21. In which district of Uttarakhand is world famous 'Valley of Flowers' is situated?
    A. Nainital   B. Uttarkashi   C. Almora   D. Chamoli

22. The main cause for the separation of Uttarakhand is–
    A. For the protection of hilly people's culture
    B. Backwardness and poverty of hilly people

C. Separate identity and land of hilly people
D. Political wish of hilly people

23. Which is the biggest district according to area of Uttarakhand?
A. Uttarkashi   B. Rudra Prayag
C. Chamoli   D. Almora

24. The Chief Minister who constituted 'Kaushik Committee' for Uttarakhand was—
A. Kalyan Singh   B. Mulayam Singh Yadav
C. Ms. Mayawati   D. Ram Prasad Gupta

25. 'Kaushik Committee' was constituted in—
A. 1994   B. 1995   C. 1996   D. 1998

26. Which district of Uttarakhand is the biggest in population?
A. Nainital   B. Chamoli   C. Haridwar   D Bageshwar

27. Which district of Uttarakhand has smallest area?
A. Dehradun   B. Uttarkashi   C. Tehri-Garhwal D. Champawat

28. The ill-famed place where inhuman atrocities were done on agitators going to New Delhi on 1-2 October, 1994.
A. Ghaziabad   B. Meerut   C. Muzaffarnagar D. New Delhi

29. What is the ancient name of Uttarakhand?
A. Dronpur   B. Brahmpur
C. Mayapur   D. Devpur

30. The students participated first time in a movement for separate Uttarakhand on—
A. July, 1992   B. July, 1993   C. July, 1994   D. July, 1995

31. The first Prime Minister who announced for separate State Uttarakhand on Independence Day is—
A. Rajeev Gandhi   B. H. D. Dev Gowda
C. Chandra Shekhar   D. Atal Bihari Vajpai

32. In which city of Uttarakhand is National Indian Military College is situated?
A. Dehradun   B. Nainital   C. Rishikesh   D. Pithoragarh

33. The Government which sent 'Uttarakhand State Bill' to U.P. State Legislative Assembly for consideration through President is—
A. Congress Govt.   B. Sanyukta Morcha Govt.
C. BJP Govt.   D. None of these

34. The President signed on 'U.P. Reconstitution Bill 2000' on—
A. 25th August, 2000   B. 26th August, 2000
C. 28th August, 2000   D. 31st August, 2000

35. Which one is the oldest Engineering University of Uttarakhand?
A. G.B. Pant University of Agriculture and Technology
B. Forest Research Institute
C. Garhwal University
D. Roorkee University

36. The motherly State of newly formed Uttarakhand is—
A. Madhya Pradesh   B. Uttar Pradesh
C. Bihar   D. Rajasthan

37. To which one is related with Lal Bahadur Shashtri Academy, Mussourie situated in Uttarakhand?
A. I.A.S. Training   B. Forest research
C. I.P.S. Training   D. Atomic Research

38. The special significance of Uttarakhand is its—
A. population   B. hilly culture
C. natural beauty   D. prosperity

39. Where is the office of Indian Survey Department situated in Uttarakhand?
A. Chamoli   B. Nainital   C. Haridwar   D. Dehradun

40. The very dense forest area of Uttarakhand is—
A. 6860 km^2 B. 4,969 km^2 C. 2086 km^2 D. 3078 km^2

41. In which city of Uttarakhand is State Forest Service College situated?
A. Almora   B. Haridwar   C. Champawat   D. Dehradun

42. The physical feature of Uttarakhand is—
A. 27° 52' N to 30° 27' N latitudes and 76° 34' E to 80° 5' E longitudes
B. 28° 43' N to 31° 27' N latitudes and 77° 35' E to 81° 02' E longitudes
C. 28° 53' N to 31° 29' N latitudes and 77° 35' E to 81° 5' E longitudes
D. 29° 52' N to 32° 29' N latitudes and 78° 36' E to 82° 6' E longitudes

43. Where is 'Indian Drugs and Pharmaceuticals Corporation' situated in Uttarakhand?
A. Rishikesh   B. Mussourie   C. Haridwar   D. Roorkee

44. The physical boundaries of Uttarakhand is—
A. Nepal and Himachal Pradesh in North, Haryana in East, U.P. in south, Himachal Pradesh and Nepal in west
B. China and Nepal in North, U.P. in East, Himachal Pradesh in south, U.P. and H.P. in west
C. U.P. and China in North, Nepal in East, H.P. in south, Haryana and H.P. in west
D. H.P. and China in North, Nepal in East, U.P. in south, Haryana and H.P. in west

45. Which institute provided the programme 'From Laboratory to Field' to give practical shape to Agriculture Policy in Uttarakhand?
    A. Chandrashekhar Azad Agriculture University
    B. Narendradev Agriculture University
    C. Pant Nagar University
    D. Raja Balwant Singh University of Agriculture

46. Uttarakhand High Court is situated at–
    A. Mussourie   B. Nainital   C. Dehradun   D. Gopeshwar

47. On which hilly place is famous Kempty Fall situated?
    A. Mussourie   B. Nainital   C. Almora   D. Lansdowne

48. The order of Uttarakhand High Court in the country's High Courts is–
    A. 18th   B. 19th.   C. 20th   D. 21st

49. In which city was situated the Summer Capital of U.P. during the British rule?
    A. Srinagar   B. Mussourie   C. Ranikhet   D. Nainital

50. The population of Uttarakhand State is according to the census of 2011–
    A. 1,50,48,560   B. 1,00,86,292   C. 90,09,280   D. 95,37,970

51. According to the census of 2011, the population density of Uttarakhand is–
    A. 189 persons per sq. km.   B. 200 persons per sq. km.
    C. 175 persons per sq. km   D. 210 persons per sq. km.

52. Where is Har-Ki-Pauri situated in Uttarakhand?
    A. Badrinath   B. Rishikesh   C. Haridwar   D. None of these

53. According to the census 2011, the literacy of Uttarakhand is–
    A. 85.48%   B. 76.38%   C. 78.8%   D. 75.18%

54. Which city of Uttarakhand was the place for the Re-establishment of Hindu Religion by Shankaracharya?
    A. Rishikesh   B. Badrinath   C. Kedarnath   D. Haridwar

55. The tillable land of Uttarakhand is–
    A. 11.5%   B. 13.06%   C. 12.5%   D. 14.5%

56. In which city of Uttarakhand is Sahastradhara waterfalls situated?
    A. Nainital   B. Almora   C. Haridwar   D. Dehradun

57. The number of seats for Parliament from Uttarakhand is–
    A. 5   B. 7   C. 8   D. 9

58. Where is Tapovan situated in Uttarakhand?
    A. Near Haridwar   B. Near Rishikesh
    C. Near Mussourie   D. Near Almora

59. The number of seats for Rajyasabha from Uttarakhand is–
A. 2   B. 3   C. 4   D. 5

60. In which district of Uttarakhand is the world famous 'Jim Corbett National Park' situated?
A. Pithoragarh   B. Chamoli   C. Nainital   D. Almora

61. The number of elected members of Uttarakhand Legislative Assembly is–
A. 40   B. 50   C. 60   D. 70

62. Where is the 'Building Research Institute and Structural Engineering Centre'?
A. Dehradun   B. Pauri
C. Narendranagar   D. Roorkee

63. In which district is the Askote Sanctuary situated?
A. Pithoragarh   B. Haridwar
C. Chamoli   D. Uttarkashi

64. Where are the highest tribal people found?
A. Chamoli   B. Udham Singh Nagar
C. Tehri-Garhwal   D. Uttarkashi

65. Uttarakhand State Council of Educational Research and Training is situated in–
A. Rishikesh   B. Mussourie
C. Narendra Nagar   D. Haridwar

66. Which pair is correct in the following given pairs?
A. Tharu-Uttarkashi   B. Jaunsar-Nainital
C. Tharu-Pithoragarh   D. Bhotia-Almora

67. The first Chief Minister of Uttarakhand Mr. Nityanand Swami was holding the post prior to it was–
A. Member of Parliament
B. Speaker of the U.P. Legislative Assembly
C. Advocate
D. Chairman of U.P. Legislative Council

68. Who was from Uttarakhand held the post of Chief Ministership of U.P. for the longest time?
A. Mr. N.D. Tiwari   B. Govind Vallabh Pant
C. Hemawati Nandan Bahuguna   D. None of these

69. Which place in Uttarakhand is called 'The Queen of the Hills'?
A. Mussourie   B. Ranikhet
C. Lansdowne   D. Nainital

70. The working field of famous leader Mr. Sunderlal Bahuguna is–
A. Social reform   B. Politics   C. Environment D. Literature

71. The highest dam of Uttarakhand is–
A. Tehri (on Bhagirathi river)   B. Kisau (Tonse river)
C. Lakhwar (Yamuna river)   D. Ramganga (Ramganga river)

72. Who was the Vice-Chancellor of Kumaon University among these?
A. Mr. Nathu Ram Upreti   B. Mr. M.D. Upadhyay
C. Mr. Baladutta Pandey   D. Mr. Chandralal Shah

73. Where is the biggest telescope of Asia having diameter of 3 metre situated in Uttarakhand?
A. Pithoragarh   B. Almora
C. Devasthal Nainital   D. Tehri-Garhwal

74. The first Chief Justice of Uttarakhand High Court was–
A. Justice S.K. Sen   B. Justice P.C. Verma
C. Justice M.C. Jain   D. Justice A.A. Desai

75. Where is 'Wild Animals Protection Training Centre' situated in Uttarakhand?
A. Kalagarh   B. Lalitpur   C. Nainital   D. Almora

76. In which field is Dr. Islam Ahmed Siddiqui famous?
A. Science   B. Politics   C. Film   D. Social work

77. The first National Park of South East Asia was Helley National Park. Now its present name is–
A. Rajajee National Park   B. Govind National Park
C. Jim Corbett National Park   D. Dudhwa National Park

78. Cabinet Minister Satpal Maharaj is originally–
A. Environmentalist   B. Litterateur
C. Politician   D. Spiritual Guru

79. In which district of Uttarakhand is Kedarnath situated?
A. Rudra Prayag   B. Uttarkashi   C. Chamoli   D. Pithoragarh

80. Who is called Kumaon Kesri in Uttarakhand?
A. Pt. Govind Vallabh Pant   B. Badri Prasad Pandey
C. Dr. Murli Manohar Joshi   D. Hemawati Nandan Bahuguna

81. Chipko Movement is related to–
A. Wildlife conservation   B. Water conservation
C. Forest conservation   D. Air conservation

82. The first Registrar General of Uttarakhand High Court was–
A. Sudhanshu Dhoolia   B. L.P. Naithani
C. M.M. Ghildiyal   D. G.C.S. Rawat

83. Tiger Project is related to–
   A. Jim Corbett National Park   B. Rajajee National Park
   C. Dudhwa National Park   D. Nanda Devi National Park

84. The first plan of Child Development is in force at–
   A. Gopeshwar   B. Bageshwar   C. Haldwani   D. Nainital

85. Whose temple is at Kedarnath?
   A. Tridev   B. Lord Vishnu   C. Lord Shiva   D Lord Brahma

86. 'Small Kashmir' is called in the State to–
   A. Almora   B. Nainital   C. Mussourie   D. Pithoragarh

87. In which city of Uttarakhand is situated the factory of Antibiotics drugs established with the help of Russia?
   A. Rishikesh   B. Nainital   C. Almora   D. Bageshwar

88. 'Forest City' in the State is called to–
   A. Uttarkashi   B. Dehradun   C. Ranikhet   D. Pauri-Garhwal

89. In which district of Uttarakhand is the cultivation of saffron done?
   A. Pithoragarh   B. Dehradun   C. Pauri-Garhwal   D. Almora

90. The economy of Uttarakhand is called–
   A. Lending Economy   B. Permanent Economy
   C. Money-order Economy   D. Temporary Economy

91. Where is Dev Sanskriti University situated?
   A. At Badrinath   B. At Kedarnath
   C. At Nainital   D. At Haridwar

92. A new aerodrome in the State is proposed at–
   A. Bajpur   B. Bageshwar   C. Gopeshwar   D. Champawat

93. Which is the second state language of Uttarakhand?
   A. Urdu   B. Sanskrit
   C. English   D. Punjabi

94. The growth rate of population of Uttarakhand State in a decade (2001-2011) is–
   A. 23.55%   B. 20.55%   C. 18.81%   D. 21.55%

95. The historical achievement of Mountaineer Bachhendri Pal is–
   A. Victory over Mount Black   B. Guidance to new Mountaineers
   C. Victory Kamet and Gameen   D. Victory over Mount Everest

96. Famous sportsman Saiyad Ali is related to–
   A. Hockey   B. Badminton   C. Tennis   D. Wrestling

97. The famous personality of the State Dr. Devidutta Pant is a–
A. Litterateur
B. Scientist
C. Public Leader
D. Social reformer

98. The permanent pasturage in Uttarakhand is–
A. 3.25%
B. 3.49%
C. 5.25%
D. 6.25%

99. According to the census 2011, the sex-ratio of Uttarakhand is–
A. 955
B. 975
C. 963
D. 970

100. The famous shooter Jaspal Rana got 8 gold medals. What was the name of that sports competition?
A. Asian Games
B. Olympic Games
C. National Games
D. Commonwealth Games

101. Which kind of fruits is produced in Uttarakhand?
A. Fruits of dry climate
B. Fruits of equable sub-tropical climate
C. Fruits of sub-tropical climate
D. Fruits of hot climate

102. Where is Tehri Dam Project situated?
A. Nainital
B. Tehri
C. Pithoragarh
D. Almora

103. At which place is Kempty waterfalls situated in Uttarakhand?
A. Nainital
B. Tehri
C. Pithoragarh
D. Almora

104. Which National Park/wildlife sanctuary has been chosen for 'Tiger Project' in the State of Uttarakhand?
A. Cheela Wildlife Sanctuary
B. Jim Corbett National Park
C. Rajajee Wildlife Sanctuary
D. Nanda Devi National Park

105. In which district of Uttarakhand is Govind Wildlife Sanctuary situated?
A. In Almora district
B. In Uttarkashi district
C. In Pithoragarh district
D. In Nainital district

106. In which year was 'The Valley of Flowers National Park' near Badrinath established?
A. 1971
B. 1981
C. 1988
D. 1978

107. When was 'Jim Corbett National Park' situated at Nainital established?
A. 1935
B. 1984
C. 1938
D. 1945

108. When was 'Forest School of Dehradun' established?
A. 1975
B. 1985
C. 1978
D. 1928

109. Who founded the 'Pashupatinath Mahadev Mandir' near Haridwar?
A. Shree Ballabhacharya
B. Baba Shravan Nath
C. King of Jammu Suchet Singh
D. Adi Shankaracharya

110. Where is the famous 'Daksheshwar Mahadev Temple' in the State?
  A. Kankhal (Haridwar)   B. Nainital
  C. Almora   D. Rishikesh

111. In which city of Uttarakhand is famous 'Ganga Mandir' situated?
  A. Haridwar   B. Almora   C. Gangotri   D. Nainital

112. Who founded the 'Badrinath Temple' in the State?
  A. Goswami Tulsidas   B. Ballabhacharya
  C. Radhaswami   D. Adi Shankaracharya

113. Which is the famous 'Musical Dance' of Garhwal region of Uttarakhand?
  A. Khayal musical-dance   B. Jhumailo musical-dance
  C. Ghuria musical-dance   D. Kartik musical dance

114. To which tribe of Uttarakhand do the sub-tribes- Katharia and Rana belong?
  A. Buxa   B. Jaunsari   C. Mahigeer   D. Tharu

115. Which tribe live in Almora, Pithoragarh, Chamoli and Uttarkashi of Uttarakhand?
  A. Buxa   B. Rajee   C. Bhotia   D. Tharu

116. Of which tribe of people worship Gawla and Bang Rang Chim gods?
  A. Tharu   B. Jaunsari   C. Bhotia   D. Rajee

117. Of which tribe of Uttarakhand does the musical instrument Hudke belong?
  A. Bhotia   B. Rajee or Banraut
  C. Buxa   D. Tharu

118. Which tribe worships the god 'Mahasu'?
  A. Tharu   B. Rajee or Banraut
  C. Buxa   D. Jaunsari

119. The famous pilgrimage of Jaunsari tribe of Uttarakhand is–
  A. Devgarh   B. Lakhamandal
  C. Kotdwar   D. Uttarkashi

120. Which tribe lives in the districts of Uttarkashi, Dehradun and Tehri-Garhwal?
  A. Tharu   B. Buxa   C. Jaunsari   D. Rajee

121. In which tribe is polyandry prevalent?
  A. Buxa   B. Tharu   C. Jaunsari   D. Bhotia

122. Which tribe of Uttarakhand worships 'Baghnath' as god?
  A. Rajee   B. Jaunsari   C. Tharu   D. Bhotia

123. In which tribe is 'Munda' language prevalent?
  A. Bhotia   B. Rajee   C. Tharu   D. Buxa

124. In which type of family system is prevalent in Tharu tribe?
- A. United System
- B. Limited System
- C. Both 'A' and 'B'
- D. None of these

125. Which city of Uttarakhand is situated on the highest altitude?
- A. Pithoragarh
- B. Nainital
- C. Tehri-Garhwal
- D. Mussourie

126. Which is the deepest lake of Uttarakhand in the following?
- A. Sat-tal Lake
- B. Khurpatal Lake
- C. Naukuchia Tal Lake
- D. Bhimtal Lake

127. In which city of Uttarakhand is 'Foundry Forge' established?
- A. Almora
- B. Chamoli
- C. Pithoragarh
- D. Haridwar

128. In which district of Uttarakhand is 'Kalsi' situated?
- A. Nainital
- B. Chamoli
- C. Pithoragarh
- D. Dehradun

129. In which city of Uttarakhand was done by Shankaracharya 'The Re-establishment of Hindu Religion'?
- A. Haridwar
- B. Badrinath
- C. Kedarnath
- D. Chamoli

130. In which of following pilgrimage is situated in Almora district?
- A. Lakhamandal
- B. Katarmal
- C. Baijnath
- D. Dwarhat

131. Where is the famous 'Surya Mandir' situated?
- A. Kausani-district-Almora
- B. Kalsi-district-Almora
- C. Katarmal-district Almora
- D. Har-Ki-Pauri-district-Haridwar

132. Which district of the State is situated in the farthest?
- A. Chamoli
- B. Pithoragarh
- C. Uttarkashi
- D. Dehradun

133. Which city of the state is known as 'Sant Nagari'?
- A. Haridwar
- B. Pithoragarh
- C. Uttarkashi
- D. Rishikesh

134. On whose consultation does the President of India appoint the Chief Justice of the State High Court?
- A. On the consultation of the Chief Justice of the Supreme Court and the Governor of the State
- B. The Governor and the Chief Minister of the State
- C. The Chief Minister and the Chief Justice of the Supreme Court
- D. The Prime Minister and the Governor of the State

135. What is the retirement age of the Chief Justice of the State High Court?
- A. 65 years
- B. 58 years
- C. 62 years
- D. 60 years

136. To whom the right to use all the executive powers is given by the Constitution?
- A. To the Council of Ministers
- B. To Governor
- C. To the C.M.
- D. To the Legislative Assembly

137. Who is popularly known as 'Gumani Kavi'?
   A. Govind Ballabh Pant
   B. Lok Ratna Pant
   C. Sumitra Nandan Pant
   D. Ramesh Chandra Pant

138. Who appoints the Governor of the State?
   A. Prime Minister
   B. President
   C. Chief Minister
   D. Home Minister

139. What is the service tenure of the State Governor?
   A. 5 years   B. 2 years   C. 6 years   D. 4 years

140. What is the minimum age for the post of Governor?
   A. 25 years   B. 30 years   C. 35 years   D. 50 years

141. Who appoint the Chairman of the State Public Service Commission?
   A. President
   B. Prime Minister
   C. Chief Minister
   D. Governor

142. Without whose recommendation the money bill can not be presented in the State Legislative Assembly?
   A. Home Minister
   B. Governor
   C. Chief Minister
   D. Finance Minister

143. Who is called the head of the Council of Ministers?
   A. Chief Minister
   B. Governor
   C. Home Minister
   D. Finance Minister

144. Who appoints the Chief Minister of the State?
   A. Prime Minister   B. Chief Justice   C. Governor   D. Parliament

145. When was the 'Forest Research Institute' was established at Dehradun?
   A. In 1914   B. In 1965   C. In 1985   D. In 1904

146. In which city of Uttarakhand is the Kumbha Fair held?
   A. Mussourie   B. Pithoragarh   C. Bageshwar   D. Haridwar

147. In which hilly region of Uttarakhand was the Summer Capital of U.P. established?
   A. Mussourie   B. Almora   C. Ranikhet   D. Nainital

148. In which district of Uttarakhand is the first 'Bal Vikas Yojna' executed?
   A. In Bageshwar
   B. In Gopeshwar
   C. In Haldwani
   D. In Chamoli

149. Of the following which is correctly matched?
   A. Bharat Heavy Electricals   – Dehradun
   B. Indian Institute of Petroleum   – Dehradun
   C. Foundry Forge Limited   – Nainital
   D. Electronic Industries   – Ranikhet

150. In which district of Uttarakhand is the cultivation of saffron done?

   A Almora   B Pauri-Garhwal

   C Dehradun   D Pithoragarh

ANSWERS

1	2	3	4	5	6	7	8	9	10
A	B	C	B	B	A	B	D	D	A

11	12	13	14	15	16	17	18	19	20
B	D	B	A	C	D	A	C	B	D

21	22	23	24	25	26	27	28	29	30
D	B	C	B	A	C	D	C	B	C

31	32	33	34	35	36	37	38	39	40
B	A	C	C	D	B	A	C	D	B

41	42	43	44	45	46	47	48	49	50
D	B	A	D	C	B	A	C	D	B

51	52	53	54	55	56	57	58	59	60
A	C	C	B	B	D	A	B	B	C

61	62	63	64	65	66	67	68	69	70
D	D	A	B	C	D	D	B	A	C

71	72	73	74	75	76	77	78	79	80
A	B	C	D	A	B	C	D	A	B

81	82	83	84	85	86	87	88	89	90
C	D	A	B	C	D	A	B	B	C

91	92	93	94	95	96	97	98	99	100
D	A	B	C	D	A	B	B	C	D

101	102	103	104	105	106	107	108	109	110
C	B	D	B	B	B	A	C	B	A

111	112	113	114	115	116	117	118	119	120
A	D	B	D	C	C	C	D	B	C

121	122	123	124	125	126	127	128	129	130
C	A	B	A	D	C	D	D	B	A

131	132	133	134	135	136	137	138	139	140
C	C	D	A	C	A	B	B	A	C

141	142	143	144	145	146	147	148	149	150
D	B	A	C	A	D	D	A	B	C

❖—❖—❖

1805